Statistische Methoden: Formelsammlung und Verteilungstabellen

Prof. Dr. Florian Heiß
HHU Düsseldorf

Statistische Methoden:

Formelsammlung und Verteilungstabellen

© Prof. Dr. Florian Heiß, 2018

HHU Düsseldorf
Universitätsstraße 1, Geb. 24.31.01.24
40225 Düsseldorf

ISBN: 978-1-7270-5665-5

Statistische Methoden: Formelsammlung und Verteilungstabellen

Prof. Dr. Florian Heiß
HHU Düsseldorf

Inhaltsverzeichnis

1 Deskriptive Statistik   **2**
  1.1 Häufigkeitsverteilung und Maßzahlen 2
  1.2 Multivariate Verteilungen 3

2 Wahrscheinlichkeitsrechnung   **4**
  2.1 Grundlagen der Wahrscheinlichkeitstheorie 4
  2.2 Zufallsvariablen 5
  2.3 Multivariate Zufallsverteilungen 6

3 Induktive Statistik   **6**
  3.1 Stichproben 6
  3.2 Asymptotik 7
  3.3 Punktschätzung 7
  3.4 Schwankungs- und Konfidenzintervalle 7
  3.5 Tests 8

4 Lineare Regression   **9**
  4.1 Lineare Einfachregression 9
  4.2 Regressionsmodell in der induktiven Statistik 9

5 Wichtige Zufallsverteilungen   **10**
  5.1 Übersicht und Eigenschaften 10
  5.2 Binomialverteilung: Verteilungsfunktion $F_{Bi}(x; p, n)$ 11
  5.3 Standardnormalverteilung: Verteilungsfunktion $F_\mathcal{N}(q; 0, 1) = \Phi(z)$ 14
  5.4 Standardnormalverteilung: Quantilsfunktion $Q_\mathcal{N}(q; 0, 1) = \Phi^{-1}(q)$ 15
  5.5 χ^2-Verteilung: Quantilsfunktion $Q_{\chi^2}(q; n)$ 16
  5.6 t-Verteilung: Quantilsfunktion $Q_t(q; n)$ 18

6 R Befehle   **20**
  6.1 Grundlegende R Befehle 20
  6.2 Beispiel-Code für Monte-Carlo Simulation 21
  RStudio Cheatsheet für `ggplot2` 22
  RStudio Cheatsheet für `dplyr` 24
  RStudio Cheatsheet für R Markdown 26

1 Deskriptive Statistik

1.1 Häufigkeitsverteilung und Maßzahlen

Statistische Verteilungen

Absolute Häufigkeit	$n_i = \text{absH}(X = x_i)$
Relative & kumulative Häufigkeit	$h_i = \text{relH}(X = x_i) = \frac{n_i}{n}, \quad H_i = \text{relH}(X \leq x_i)$
Häufigkeits- & Verteilungsfunktion	$h(x) = \text{relH}(X = x), \quad H(x) = \text{relH}(X \leq x)$
Intervalle	$H(b) - H(a) = \text{relH}(a < X \leq b)$
Histogramm: Klassenbreite Klasse i	$b_i = g_i - g_{i-1} \quad$ mit Klassengrenzen $g_0, g_1, g_2, \ldots, g_m$
Klassenhäufigkeit	$h_i = \text{relH}(g_{i-1} < X \leq g_i)$
Häufigkeitsdichte	$\overline{h}(x) = \frac{h_i}{b_i}$ für $g_{i-1} < x \leq g_i$
Quantile	$x[q] = \min\{x \mid H(x) \geq q\}, \quad$ für $x_1 \leq \ldots \leq x_n$: $x[q] = x_{\lceil nq \rceil}$

Maßzahlen

Arithmetisches Mittel	$\bar{x} = \frac{1}{n} \sum_{j=1}^{n} x_j \quad$ (falls $x_1, x_2, \ldots, x_n$ gegeben) $\bar{x} = \frac{1}{n} \sum_{j=1}^{k} n_j x_j = \sum_{j=1}^{k} h_j x_j \quad$ (falls Häufigkeiten gegeben)
Median für $x_1 \leq \ldots \leq x_i \leq \ldots \leq x_n$:	$x_{\text{Med}} = \min\{x \mid H(x) \geq \frac{1}{2}\}$ $\begin{array}{c\|cc} & n \text{ ungerade} & n \text{ gerade} \\ \hline x_{\text{Med}} & x_{\frac{n+1}{2}} & x_{\frac{n}{2}} \\ x^*_{\text{Med}} & x_{\frac{n+1}{2}} & \frac{1}{2}\left(x_{\frac{n}{2}} + x_{\frac{n}{2}+1}\right) \end{array}$
Modus	$h(x_{\text{Mod}}) \geq h(x_i)$ für alle i
Geometrisches Mittel	$x_{\text{Geo}} = \sqrt[n]{x_1 \cdot x_2 \cdot \ldots \cdot x_n}$ mit $x_i > 0$
Harmonisches Mittel	$x_{\text{Har}} = \dfrac{1}{\frac{1}{n} \sum_{j=1}^{n} \frac{1}{x_j}}$ mit $x_j > 0$
Spannweite	$r_X = \max(X) - \min(X)$
Mittlere absolute Abweichung	$MAA = \frac{1}{n} \sum_{j=1}^{n} |x_j - \bar{x}|$
Interquartilsabstand	$IQA = Q_3 - Q_1$
Mittlerer Quartilsabstand	$MQA = \dfrac{IQA}{2}$
(Unkorrigierte) Varianz	$s_X^2 = \frac{1}{n} \sum_{j=1}^{n} (x_j - \bar{x})^2 \quad (x_1, x_2, \ldots, x_n$ gegeben) $\quad = \frac{1}{n} \sum_{j=1}^{n} x_j^2 - \bar{x}^2 = \overline{x^2} - \bar{x}^2$ $s_X^2 = \frac{1}{n} \sum_{j=1}^{k} n_j (x_j - \bar{x})^2 \quad (n_i$ gegeben) $s_X^2 = \sum_{j=1}^{k} h_j (x_j - \bar{x})^2 \quad (h_i$ gegeben)
Korrigierte Varianz	$\tilde{s}_X^2 = \frac{1}{n-1} \sum_{j=1}^{n} (x_j - \bar{x})^2 = \frac{n}{n-1} s_X^2$
Standardabweichung	$s_X = \sqrt{s_X^2} \quad$ bzw. $\quad \tilde{s}_X = \sqrt{\tilde{s}_X^2}$
Varianzzerlegung	$s_{\text{ges}}^2 = \underbrace{\frac{1}{n} \sum_{j=1}^{m} n_j s_j^2}_{\text{Interne Varianz}} + \underbrace{\frac{1}{n} \sum_{j=1}^{m} n_j (\bar{x}_j - \bar{x}_{\text{ges}})^2}_{\text{Externe Varianz}}$
Variationskoeffizient	$VK_X = \dfrac{s_X}{|\bar{x}|}$

Konzentrationsmaße

Anteil von Merkmalsträgern	$H_i = \frac{i}{n}$	(für Rohdaten)
	$H_i = \sum_{j=1}^{i} h_j$	(für klassifizierte Daten)
Kummulierte Merkmalssumme	$M_i = \frac{1}{S}\left(\sum_{j=1}^{i} x_j\right)$	(für Rohdaten)
	$M_i = \frac{1}{S}\left(\sum_{j=1}^{i} n_j x_j\right)$	(für klassifizierte Daten)
Konzentrationsfläche	$KF = \frac{1}{2} - \sum_{i=1}^{k} h_i \cdot \frac{1}{2}(M_{i-1} + M_i)$	
Gini-Koeffizient	$GINI = 2KF = 1 - \sum_{i=1}^{k} h_i \cdot (M_{i-1} + M_i)$	
Korrigierter Gini	$GINI_{korr} = \frac{n}{n-1} \cdot GINI$	

1.2 Multivariate Verteilungen

Gemeinsame Verteilung

Absolute gemeinsame Häufigkeiten	$n_{ij} = \text{absH}(X=x_i \cap Y=y_j)$	mit $i=1,...,k$, $j=1,...,l$
Relative gemeinsame Häufigkeiten	$h_{ij} = \text{relH}(X=x_i \cap Y=y_j) = \frac{n_{ij}}{n}$	mit $i=1,...,k$, $j=1,...,l$
Absolute Randhäufigkeiten	$n_{i\cdot} = \text{absH}(X=x_i) = \sum_{j=1}^{l} n_{ij}, \quad n_{\cdot j} = \text{absH}(Y=y_j) = \sum_{i=1}^{k} n_{ij}$	
Relative Randhäufigkeiten	$h_{i\cdot} = \text{relH}(X=x_i) = \frac{n_{i\cdot}}{n}, \quad h_{\cdot j} = \text{relH}(Y=y_j) = \frac{n_{\cdot j}}{n}$	
Bedingte Häufigkeiten	$\text{relH}(X=x_i|Y=y_j) = h_{i|y_j} = \frac{n_{ij}}{n_{\cdot j}} = \frac{h_{ij}}{h_{\cdot j}}$	
	$\text{relH}(Y=y_j|X=x_i) = h_{j|x_i} = \frac{n_{ij}}{n_{i\cdot}} = \frac{h_{ij}}{h_{i\cdot}}$	
Statistische Unabhängigkeit	$h_{ij} = \text{relH}(X=x_i) \cdot \text{relH}(Y=y_j) = h_{i\cdot} \cdot h_{\cdot j}$	
	$\Leftrightarrow \quad \text{relH}(Y=y_j|X=x_i) = \text{relH}(Y=y_j)$	
Bedingter Mittelwert	$\bar{y}|x_i = \sum_{j=1}^{l} h_{j|x_i} \cdot y_j$	
Bedingte Varianz	$s_Y^2|x_i = \sum_{j=1}^{l} h_{j|x_i} \cdot (y_j - (\bar{y}|x_i))^2$	

Zusammenhangsmaße

(Unkorrigierte) Kovarianz	$c_{XY} = \frac{1}{n}\sum_{j=1}^{n}(x_j - \bar{x})(y_j - \bar{y})$	
	$\quad\quad = \overline{xy} - \bar{x}\bar{y}$	$((x_i, y_i)$, mit $i=1,...,n$ gegeben)
	$c_{XY} = \frac{1}{n}\sum_{i=1}^{k}\sum_{j=1}^{l} n_{ij}(x_i - \bar{x})(y_j - \bar{y})$	(n_{ij} gegeben)
	$c_{XY} = \sum_{i=1}^{k}\sum_{j=1}^{l} h_{ij}(x_i - \bar{x})(y_j - \bar{y})$	(h_{ij} gegeben)
Korrigierte Kovarianz	$\tilde{c}_{XY} = \frac{1}{n-1}\sum_{j=1}^{n}(x_j - \bar{x})(y_j - \bar{y}) = \frac{n}{n-1} c_{XY}$	
Korrelationskoeffizient	$r_{XY} = \dfrac{c_{XY}}{s_X \cdot s_y} = \dfrac{\tilde{c}_{XY}}{\tilde{s}_X \cdot \tilde{s}_Y}$	
Rangkorrelation	$r_{XY}^{Sp} = r_{\text{rg}(X),\text{rg}(Y)}$	
Quadratische Kontingenz	$QK = \sum_{i=1}^{k}\sum_{j=1}^{l} \dfrac{(n_{ij} - E_{ij})^2}{E_{ij}} \quad \text{mit } E_{ij} = n \cdot h_{i\cdot} \cdot h_{\cdot j} = \dfrac{n_{i\cdot} \cdot n_{\cdot j}}{n}$	
Korrigierter Kontingenzkoeffizient	$KK^* = \sqrt{\dfrac{QK \cdot m}{(QK+n)(m-1)}} \quad$ wobei $m = \min(k,l)$	

Sonstiges

Gewichtete Summe	$z_i = b_1 x_i + b_2 y_i \;\Rightarrow\; \bar{z} = b_1 \bar{x} + b_2 \bar{y}$ $\Rightarrow\; s_Z^2 = b_1^2 s_X^2 + b_2^2 s_Y^2 + 2 b_1 b_2 c_{XY}$
Lineare Transformationen	$U = a_1 + b_1 X, \quad V = a_2 + b_2 Y$ $c_{UV} = b_1 b_2 c_{XY}, \quad \tilde{c}_{UV} = b_1 b_2 \tilde{c}_{XY}$ $r_{UV} = \begin{cases} r_{XY} & \text{wenn } b_1 b_2 > 0 \\ -r_{XY} & \text{wenn } b_1 b_2 < 0 \end{cases}$

2 Wahrscheinlichkeitsrechnung

2.1 Grundlagen der Wahrscheinlichkeitstheorie

Bedingte Wahrscheinlichkeiten	$P(A|B) = \frac{P(A \cap B)}{P(B)}$
Stochastische Unabhängigkeit	
$\quad$ von Ereignissen A und B	$P(A|B) = P(A) \quad \text{bzw.} \quad P(B|A) = P(B)$ $\Leftrightarrow P(A \cap B) = P(A) \cdot P(B)$
$\quad$ von Ereignissen $A_1, A_2, \ldots, A_n$	$P(A_{i_1} \cap A_{i_2} \cap \cdots \cap A_{i_k}) = P(A_{i_1}) \cdot P(A_{i_2}) \cdot \ldots \cdot P(A_{i_k})$
Totale Wahrscheinlichkeit	Mit Partition $H_1, \ldots H_n$: $\quad P(A) = \sum_{j=1}^n P(A|H_j) \cdot P(H_j)$
Bayes-Theorem	$P(A|B) = P(B|A) \dfrac{P(A)}{P(B)}$
Permutationen	$_n P = n \cdot (n-1) \cdot (n-2) \cdot \ldots \cdot 2 \cdot 1 = n!$
Kombinationen, Anordnung	
$\quad$ nicht berücksichtigt	$_n C_k = \binom{n}{k} = \dfrac{n!}{(n-k)!\,k!}$
$\quad$ berücksichtigt	$_n V_k = \binom{n}{k} k! = \dfrac{n!}{(n-k)!} = n \cdot (n-1) \cdot (n-2) \cdot \ldots \cdot (n-k+1)$

2.2 Zufallsvariablen

Allgemeine Eigenschaften

Verteilungsfunktion und Wahrscheinlichkeiten	$P(X \leq x) = F_X(x)$ $P(X > x) = 1 - P(X \leq x) = 1 - F_X(x)$ $P(a < X \leq b) = F_X(b) - F_X(a)$
Stetige ZV: Verteilungsfunktion	$F_X(x) = \int_{-\infty}^{x} f_X(u)du$
Dichtefunktion	$f_X(x) = \frac{d}{dx} F_X(x) = F'_X(x)$
Quantile	$Q_X(q) = \min\{x \mid F(x) \geq q\}$ $Q_X(q) = F^{-1}(q)$ (bei streng monotoner $F(x)$)
Median	$x_{\text{med}} = Q_X(0.5) = \min\{x \mid F(x) \geq \frac{1}{2}\}$
Erwartungswert (diskrete ZV)	$\mu_X = E(X) = \sum_j x_j f(x_j)$ $E(g(X)) = \sum_j g(x_j) f(x_j)$
Erwartungswert (stetige ZV)	$\mu_X = E(X) = \int_{-\infty}^{\infty} x f(x)dx$ $E(g(X)) = \int_{-\infty}^{\infty} g(x) f(x)dx$
Rechenregeln für den Erwartungswert	$E(a + bX) = a + bE(X)$ $E(g_1(X) + g_2(X)) = E(g_1(X)) + E(g_2(X))$
Varianz und Standardabweichung	$\sigma_X^2 = V(X) = E((X - \mu_X)^2) = E(X^2) - \mu_X^2$ $\sigma_X = \sqrt{V(X)}$
Rechenregeln für die Varianz	$V(a + bX) = b^2 V(X)$
Momente: nicht-zentral	$M_k = E(X^k)$
zentral	$M_k^Z = E\left((X - \mu)^k\right)$
Schiefe	$\gamma = \dfrac{M_3^Z}{\sigma^3} = \dfrac{E(X - \mu)^3}{\sigma^3}$
Wölbung (Kurtosis)	$\kappa = \dfrac{M_4^Z}{\sigma^4} = \dfrac{E(X - \mu)^4}{\sigma^4}$

Standardisierung

Standardisieren einer Variable X	$Z = \frac{X-\mu}{\sigma}$
Verteilungsfunktion	$F_Z(z) = F_X(z\sigma + \mu)$ $\quad$ $F_X(x) = F_Z\left(\frac{x-\mu}{\sigma}\right)$
Wahrscheinlichkeitsmassenfunktion	$f_Z(z) = f_X(z\sigma + \mu)$ $\quad$ $f_X(x) = f_Z\left(\frac{x-\mu}{\sigma}\right)$
Wahrscheinlichkeitsdichtefunktion	$f_Z(z) = \sigma f_X(z\sigma + \mu)$ $\quad$ $f_X(x) = \frac{1}{\sigma} f_Z\left(\frac{x-\mu}{\sigma}\right)$

2.3 Multivariate Zufallsverteilungen

Bedingte Verteilungen	$f_X(x\mid y) = \dfrac{f(x,y)}{f_Y(y)} \quad f_Y(y\mid x) = \dfrac{f(x,y)}{f_X(x)}$
Kovarianz	$\mathrm{Cov}(X,Y) = \mathrm{E}\left((X-\mu_X)(Y-\mu_Y)\right) = \mathrm{E}(XY) - \mathrm{E}(X)\mathrm{E}(Y)$
Korrelation	$\rho_{XY} = \dfrac{\mathrm{Cov}(X,Y)}{\sigma_X \cdot \sigma_Y}$
Stochastische Unabhängigkeit von X und Y: für alle x,y	$f_X(x\mid y) = f_X(x) \;\Leftrightarrow\; f_Y(y\mid x) = f_Y(y)$ $\Leftrightarrow f(x,y) = f_X(x)f_Y(y)$ $\Rightarrow \mathrm{Cov}(X,Y) = 0$
Rechenregeln: Erwartungswert	$\mathrm{E}(aX + bY) = a\mathrm{E}(X) + b\mathrm{E}(Y)$
Varianz	$\mathrm{V}(aX + bY) = a^2\mathrm{V}(X) + b^2\mathrm{V}(Y) + 2ab\,\mathrm{Cov}(X,Y)$
Kovarianz	$\mathrm{Cov}(aX+bY, cU+dV) = ac\,\mathrm{Cov}(X,U) + ad\,\mathrm{Cov}(X,V)$ $+ bc\,\mathrm{Cov}(Y,U) + bd\,\mathrm{Cov}(Y,V)$

3 Induktive Statistik

3.1 Stichproben

Stichprobenmittelwert mit $\mathrm{E}(X)=\mu,\ \mathrm{V}(X)=\sigma^2$	$\overline{X}_n = \dfrac{1}{n}\sum_{i=1}^{n} X_i$ $\mu_{\overline{X}_n} = \mathrm{E}\left(\overline{X}_n\right) = \mu$ $\sigma^2_{\overline{X}_n} = \dfrac{\sigma^2}{n} \qquad \sigma_{\overline{X}_n} = \dfrac{\sigma}{\sqrt{n}}$ $X_i \sim \mathcal{N}(\mu,\sigma^2) \;\Rightarrow\; \overline{X}_n \sim \mathcal{N}\left(\mu, \dfrac{\sigma^2}{n}\right)$
Unkorrigierte Stichprobenvarianz	$S_X^2 = \dfrac{1}{n}\sum_{i=1}^{n}\left(X_i - \overline{X}_n\right)^2 = \overline{X_i^2} - \overline{X}_n^2$ $\mathrm{E}\left(S_X^2\right) = \dfrac{n-1}{n}\sigma^2$
Korrigierte Stichprobenvarianz	$\tilde{S}_X^2 = \dfrac{1}{n-1}\sum_{i=1}^{n}\left(X_i - \overline{X}_n\right)^2 = \dfrac{n}{n-1}S_X^2$ $\mathrm{E}\left(\tilde{S}_X^2\right) = \sigma^2$ $X \sim \mathcal{N}(\mu,\sigma^2) \;\Rightarrow\; (n-1)\dfrac{\tilde{S}_X^2}{\sigma^2} \sim \chi^2_{n-1}$

3.2 Asymptotik

Hauptsatz der Statistik	$P\left(\lim_{n\to\infty} H_n(x) = F(x)\right) = 1$
Gesetz der großen Zahlen (GGZ)	$\lim_{n\to\infty} P\left(\|\overline{X}_n - \mu\| \geq \varepsilon\right) \to 0 \quad$ für jedes $\varepsilon > 0$ $\Leftrightarrow \quad \text{plim}\,\overline{X}_n = \mu \quad \Leftrightarrow \quad \overline{X}_n \xrightarrow{p} \mu$
GGZ für Funktionen	$\text{plim}\left(g(\overline{X}_n)\right) = g\left(\text{plim}(\overline{X}_n)\right)$
Zentraler Grenzwertsatz (ZGS)	$Z_n = \dfrac{\overline{X}_n - E(\overline{X}_n)}{\sqrt{V(\overline{X}_n)}} = \sqrt{n}\,\dfrac{\overline{X}_n - \mu}{\sigma}$ $\Rightarrow \lim_{n\to\infty} F_{Z_n}(z) \to \Phi(z)$ für alle $z \Leftrightarrow \quad Z_n \overset{a}{\sim} \mathcal{N}(0,1)$

3.3 Punktschätzung

Allgemeine Eigenschaften von Punktschätzern	$\hat{\theta}$ ist erwartungstreu: $\qquad E(\hat{\theta}) = \theta$ $\hat{\theta}$ ist asymptotisch erwartungstreu: $\lim_{n\to\infty} E(\hat{\theta}) = \theta$ $\hat{\theta}$ ist konsistent: $\qquad \text{plim}\,\hat{\theta} = \theta$ $\text{bias}_\theta = E(\hat{\theta}) - \theta$ $MSE(\hat{\theta}) = E\left[(\hat{\theta} - \theta)^2\right] = V(\hat{\theta}) + \text{bias}_\theta^2$
Schätzer für μ und σ^2	$\hat{\mu} = \overline{X}_n, \quad \widehat{\sigma^2} = \tilde{S}_X^2$
Varianz und Standardfehler von $\hat{\mu}$	$\sigma_{\hat{\mu}}^2 = \dfrac{\sigma^2}{n} \qquad \hat{\sigma}_{\hat{\mu}} = \sqrt{\dfrac{\widehat{\sigma^2}}{n}} = \sqrt{\dfrac{\tilde{S}_X^2}{n}} = \dfrac{\tilde{S}_X}{\sqrt{n}}$

3.4 Schwankungs- und Konfidenzintervalle

Allgemein	$SI(\hat{\theta}, 1-\alpha) = \left[Q_{\hat{\theta}}(\tfrac{\alpha}{2}); \quad Q_{\hat{\theta}}(1-\tfrac{\alpha}{2})\right]$
Symmetrische Verteilung	$SI(\hat{\theta}, 1-\alpha) = [\theta - d; \quad \theta + d]$ $KI(\theta, 1-\alpha) = [\hat{\theta} - d; \quad \hat{\theta} + d]$

Für den Erwartungswert von X	Verteilung X	σ bekannt?	n^*	d
	beliebig	ja	groß	$\Phi^{-1}(1-\tfrac{\alpha}{2}) \cdot \tfrac{\sigma}{\sqrt{n}}$
	Normalvert.	ja	beliebig	
	beliebig	nein	groß	$\Phi^{-1}(1-\tfrac{\alpha}{2}) \cdot \tfrac{\hat{\sigma}}{\sqrt{n}}$
	Normalvert.	nein	beliebig	$Q_t(1-\tfrac{\alpha}{2}; n\text{-}1) \cdot \tfrac{\hat{\sigma}}{\sqrt{n}}$

*: Daumenregel für „groß": $n > 30$

3.5 Tests

Fehler

Testentscheidung	Realität	
	H_0 ist wahr	H_0 ist falsch
H_0 beibehalten	korrekt!	Fehler 2. Art
H_0 verwerfen	Fehler 1. Art	korrekt!

Wahrscheinlichkeiten

Wahrscheinlichkeit	Gegeben	
	H_0 ist wahr	H_0 ist falsch
P(H_0 beibehalten)	$1 - \alpha$	β
P(H_0 verwerfen)	α (Signifikanzniveau)	$1 - \beta$ (Macht)

Testentscheidungen

bei einer Teststatistik mit Verteilungsfunktion $F(W)$ und Quantilsfunktion $Q(W)$

Verteilung von W	Beidseitiger Test	Oberseitiger Test	Unterseitiger Test
Ablehnungsbereiche			
Allgemein	$W < Q(\frac{\alpha}{2})$; $W > Q(1-\frac{\alpha}{2})$	$W > Q(1-\alpha)$	$W < Q(\alpha)$
Symmetrisch um 0	$\|W\| > Q(1-\frac{\alpha}{2})$		
p-Werte			
Allgemein	$p = 2 \min\{F(w), 1-F(w)\}$	$p = 1-F(w)$	$p = F(w)$
Symmetrisch um 0	$p = 2(1-F(\|w\|))$		

Die wichtigsten Teststatistiken und Verteilung unter H_0

Test	n	Verteilung	H_0	Teststatistik W	Verteilung
E(X), σ bekannt	groß	beliebig	$\mu = \mu_0$	$\sqrt{n}\dfrac{\overline{X} - \mu_0}{\sigma}$	$\mathcal{N}(0,1)$
E(X), σ bekannt	beliebig	$\mathcal{N}(\mu, \sigma^2)$	$\mu = \mu_0$	$\sqrt{n}\dfrac{\overline{X} - \mu_0}{\sigma}$	$\mathcal{N}(0,1)$
E(X), σ unbekannt	groß	beliebig	$\mu = \mu_0$	$\sqrt{n}\dfrac{\overline{X} - \mu_0}{\tilde{S}_n}$	$\mathcal{N}(0,1)$
E(X), σ unbekannt	beliebig	$\mathcal{N}(\mu, \sigma^2)$	$\mu = \mu_0$	$\sqrt{n}\dfrac{\overline{X} - \mu_0}{\tilde{S}_n}$	t_{n-1}
Wahrscheinlichkeit p	groß	Bernoulli(p)	$p = p_0$	$\sqrt{n}\dfrac{\hat{p} - p_0}{\sqrt{p_0(1-p_0)}}$	$\mathcal{N}(0,1)$
Mittelwertvergleich	groß	beliebig	$\mu_1-\mu_2=0$	$\dfrac{\overline{X}_1 - \overline{X}_2}{\sqrt{\frac{\tilde{s}_1^2}{n_1}+\frac{\tilde{s}_2^2}{n_2}}}$	$\mathcal{N}(0,1)$
χ^2-Anpassungstest	groß	beliebig	$F(x)=F_0(x)$	$\sum_{j=1}^m \dfrac{(n_j-\mathrm{E}_0(n_j))^2}{\mathrm{E}_0(n_j)}$	χ^2_{m-1}
Unabhängigkeit	groß	beliebig	Unabh.	$\sum_{i=1}^k \sum_{j=1}^m \dfrac{(n_{ij}-E_{ij})^2}{E_{ij}}$	$\chi^2_{(k-1)\cdot(m-1)}$

4 Lineare Regression

4.1 Lineare Einfachregression

Regressionsgleichung	$y_i = a + b \cdot x_i + e_i$
Kriterium	$SQA(a,b) = \sum_{j=1}^{n} e_j^2 \xrightarrow[a,b]{} Min$
Regressionskoeffizienten	$b = \frac{c_{XY}}{s_X^2} = r_{XY} \frac{s_Y}{s_X}$ und $a = \bar{y} - b\bar{x}$
Bestimmtheitsmaß	$R^2 = \frac{s_{\hat{Y}}^2}{s_Y^2} = r_{XY}^2$

4.2 Regressionsmodell in der induktiven Statistik

Annahmen	R1: $y_i = \alpha + \beta x_i + u_i$ R2: $E(u_i\|x_i) = 0$ (Erwartungswert, Unabhängigkeit) R3: $V(u_i\|x_i) = \sigma^2$ (konstante Varianz, „Homoskedastie") R4: $Cov(u_i, u_j\|x_i) = 0$ („keine Autokorrelation") R5: $u_i \sim \mathcal{N}(0, \sigma^2)$ (Normalverteilung)
Geschätzte Varianz von u	$\hat{\sigma}_u^2 = \frac{1}{n-2} \sum_{i=1}^{n} \hat{u}_i^2$
Standardfehler des Fehlerterms	$\hat{\sigma}_u = \sqrt{\hat{\sigma}_u^2}$
Standardfehler von $\hat{\beta}$	$\hat{\sigma}_{\hat{\beta}} = \frac{1}{\sqrt{n}} \cdot \frac{\hat{\sigma}_u}{S_x}$
Teststatistik für $H_0 : \beta = 0$	$t_{\hat{\beta}} = \frac{\hat{\beta}}{\hat{\sigma}_{\hat{\beta}}} \sim t_{n-2}$ unter H_0 und R1–R5

5 Wichtige Zufallsverteilungen

5.1 Übersicht und Eigenschaften

Verteilungs-, Wahrscheinlichkeitsmassen-, Dichte- und Quantilsfunktionen

Verteilung	Abk.	$f(x)$	$F(x)$	$Q(q)$
Binomial	$Bi(p,n)$	$\binom{n}{x}p^x(1-p)^{n-x}$	$\sum_{k=0}^{x} f(k)$ ⋆	
Geometrische	$Geo(p)$	$(1-p)^x p$	$1-(1-p)^{x+1}$	
Rechteckvert.	$R(a,b)$	$\frac{1}{b-a}$	$\frac{x-a}{b-a}$	$a+q(b-a)$
Logistische V.	Log	$\frac{e^{-x}}{(1+e^{-x})^2}$	$\frac{1}{1+e^{-x}}$	$\ln\left(\frac{q}{1-q}\right)$
Exponentialv.	$Ex(\lambda)$	$\lambda e^{-\lambda x}$	$1-e^{-\lambda x}$	$\frac{-\ln(1-q)}{\lambda}$
Standardnormalv.	$\mathcal{N}(0,1)$	$\phi(x) = \frac{1}{\sqrt{2\pi}}e^{-\frac{1}{2}x^2}$	$\Phi(x)$ ⋆	$\Phi^{-1}(q)$ ⋆
Normalvert.	$\mathcal{N}(\mu,\sigma^2)$	$\frac{1}{\sigma}\phi\left(\frac{x-\mu}{\sigma}\right)$	$\Phi\left(\frac{x-\mu}{\sigma}\right)$	$\Phi^{-1}(q)\cdot\sigma+\mu$
χ^2-Vert.	χ_n^2	↯	↯	↯ ⋆
t-Verteilung	t_n	↯	↯	↯ ⋆

↯: keine analytische Funktion.   ⋆: im Tabellenteil enthalten

Eigenschaften

Verteilung	Parameter	Werte	$E(X)$	$V(X)$	x_{med}
Bernoulli	p	$\{0,1\}$	p	$p(1-p)$	gerundet(p)
Binomial	p,n	$\{0,1,\ldots,n\}$	$n\cdot p$	$n\cdot p(1-p)$	abgerundet(p)
Geometrische	p	$\{0,1,\ldots\}$	$\frac{1-p}{p}$	$\frac{1-p}{p^2}$	↯
Rechteckvert.	a,b	$a \leq X \leq b$	$\frac{a+b}{2}$	$\frac{(b-a)^2}{12}$	$\frac{a+b}{2}$
Logistische V.	—	$\mathbb{R}$	0	$\frac{\pi^2}{3}$	0
Exponentialv.	λ	$X \geq 0$	$\frac{1}{\lambda}$	$\frac{1}{\lambda^2}$	$\frac{\ln(2)}{\lambda}$
Standardnormalv.	—	$\mathbb{R}$	0	1	0
Normalvert.	μ,σ^2	$\mathbb{R}$	μ	σ^2	μ
χ^2-Vert.	n	$X \geq 0$	n	$2n$	↯
t-Verteilung	n	$\mathbb{R}$	0*	$\frac{n}{n-2}$**	0

↯: kein einfacher Ausdruck.   *: für $n>1$ **: für $n>2$

R Befehle für Verteilungen

Verteilung	$f(x)$	$F(x)$	$Q(q)$	R Zufallsziehungen
Binomial	dbinom(x,n,p)	pbinom(x,n,p)	qbinom(q,n,p)	rbinom(R,n,p)
Geometr.	dgeom(x,p)	pgeom(x,p)	qgeom(q,p)	rgeom(R,p)
Rechteckvert.	dunif(x,a,b)	punif(x,a,b)	qunif(q,a,b)	runif(R,a,b)
Logistische V.	dlogis(x)	plogis(x)	qlogis(q)	rlogis(R)
Exponentialv.	dexp(x,λ)	pexp(x,λ)	qexp(q,λ)	rexp(R,λ)
Standardnormalv.	dnorm(x)	pnorm(x)	qnorm(q)	rnorm(R)
Normalvert.	dnorm(x,μ,σ)	pnorm(x,μ,σ)	qnorm(q,μ,σ)	rnorm(R,μ,σ)
χ^2-Vert.	dchisq(x,n)	pchisq(x,n)	qchisq(q,n)	rchisq(R,n)
t-Verteilung	dt(x,n)	pt(x,n)	qt(q,n)	rt(R,n)

5.2 Binomialverteilung: Verteilungsfunktion $F_{Bi}(x;p,n)$

- Für Wahrscheinlichkeiten $p > \frac{1}{2}$ gilt: $F_{Bi}(x;p,n) = 1 - F_{Bi}(n-x-1;1-p,n)$
- R Code: pbinom(x,n,p)

		\multicolumn{10}{c}{Erfolgswahrscheinlichkeit p}									
n	x	0.02	0.05	0.10	$\frac{1}{6}$	0.20	0.25	0.30	$\frac{1}{3}$	0.40	0.50
1	0	0.9800	0.9500	0.9000	0.8333	0.8000	0.7500	0.7000	0.6667	0.6000	0.5000
2	0	0.9604	0.9025	0.8100	0.6944	0.6400	0.5625	0.4900	0.4444	0.3600	0.2500
	1	0.9996	0.9975	0.9900	0.9722	0.9600	0.9375	0.9100	0.8889	0.8400	0.7500
3	0	0.9412	0.8574	0.7290	0.5787	0.5120	0.4219	0.3430	0.2963	0.2160	0.1250
	1	0.9988	0.9928	0.9720	0.9259	0.8960	0.8438	0.7840	0.7407	0.6480	0.5000
	2	1.0000	0.9999	0.9990	0.9954	0.9920	0.9844	0.9730	0.9630	0.9360	0.8750
4	0	0.9224	0.8145	0.6561	0.4823	0.4096	0.3164	0.2401	0.1975	0.1296	0.0625
	1	0.9977	0.9860	0.9477	0.8681	0.8192	0.7383	0.6517	0.5926	0.4752	0.3125
	2	1.0000	0.9995	0.9963	0.9838	0.9728	0.9492	0.9163	0.8889	0.8208	0.6875
	3	1.0000	1.0000	0.9999	0.9992	0.9984	0.9961	0.9919	0.9877	0.9744	0.9375
5	0	0.9039	0.7738	0.5905	0.4019	0.3277	0.2373	0.1681	0.1317	0.0778	0.0312
	1	0.9962	0.9774	0.9185	0.8038	0.7373	0.6328	0.5282	0.4609	0.3370	0.1875
	2	0.9999	0.9988	0.9914	0.9645	0.9421	0.8965	0.8369	0.7901	0.6826	0.5000
	3	1.0000	1.0000	0.9995	0.9967	0.9933	0.9844	0.9692	0.9547	0.9130	0.8125
	4	1.0000	1.0000	1.0000	0.9999	0.9997	0.9990	0.9976	0.9959	0.9898	0.9688
6	0	0.8858	0.7351	0.5314	0.3349	0.2621	0.1780	0.1176	0.0878	0.0467	0.0156
	1	0.9943	0.9672	0.8857	0.7368	0.6554	0.5339	0.4202	0.3512	0.2333	0.1094
	2	0.9998	0.9978	0.9842	0.9377	0.9011	0.8306	0.7443	0.6804	0.5443	0.3437
	3	1.0000	0.9999	0.9987	0.9913	0.9830	0.9624	0.9295	0.8999	0.8208	0.6562
	4	1.0000	1.0000	0.9999	0.9993	0.9984	0.9954	0.9891	0.9822	0.9590	0.8906
	5	1.0000	1.0000	1.0000	1.0000	0.9999	0.9998	0.9993	0.9986	0.9959	0.9844
7	0	0.8681	0.6983	0.4783	0.2791	0.2097	0.1335	0.0824	0.0585	0.0280	0.0078
	1	0.9921	0.9556	0.8503	0.6698	0.5767	0.4449	0.3294	0.2634	0.1586	0.0625
	2	0.9997	0.9962	0.9743	0.9042	0.8520	0.7564	0.6471	0.5706	0.4199	0.2266
	3	1.0000	0.9998	0.9973	0.9824	0.9667	0.9294	0.8740	0.8267	0.7102	0.5000
	4	1.0000	1.0000	0.9998	0.9980	0.9953	0.9871	0.9712	0.9547	0.9037	0.7734
	5	1.0000	1.0000	1.0000	0.9999	0.9996	0.9987	0.9962	0.9931	0.9812	0.9375
	6	1.0000	1.0000	1.0000	1.0000	1.0000	0.9999	0.9998	0.9995	0.9984	0.9922
8	0	0.8508	0.6634	0.4305	0.2326	0.1678	0.1001	0.0576	0.0390	0.0168	0.0039
	1	0.9897	0.9428	0.8131	0.6047	0.5033	0.3671	0.2553	0.1951	0.1064	0.0352
	2	0.9996	0.9942	0.9619	0.8652	0.7969	0.6785	0.5518	0.4682	0.3154	0.1445
	3	1.0000	0.9996	0.9950	0.9693	0.9437	0.8862	0.8059	0.7414	0.5941	0.3633
	4	1.0000	1.0000	0.9996	0.9954	0.9896	0.9727	0.9420	0.9121	0.8263	0.6367
	5	1.0000	1.0000	1.0000	0.9996	0.9988	0.9958	0.9887	0.9803	0.9502	0.8555
	6	1.0000	1.0000	1.0000	1.0000	0.9999	0.9996	0.9987	0.9974	0.9915	0.9648
	7	1.0000	1.0000	1.0000	1.0000	1.0000	1.0000	0.9999	0.9998	0.9993	0.9961
9	0	0.8337	0.6302	0.3874	0.1938	0.1342	0.0751	0.0404	0.0260	0.0101	0.0020
	1	0.9869	0.9288	0.7748	0.5427	0.4362	0.3003	0.1960	0.1431	0.0705	0.0195
	2	0.9994	0.9916	0.9470	0.8217	0.7382	0.6007	0.4628	0.3772	0.2318	0.0898
	3	1.0000	0.9994	0.9917	0.9520	0.9144	0.8343	0.7297	0.6503	0.4826	0.2539
	4	1.0000	1.0000	0.9991	0.9910	0.9804	0.9511	0.9012	0.8552	0.7334	0.5000
	5	1.0000	1.0000	0.9999	0.9989	0.9969	0.9900	0.9747	0.9576	0.9006	0.7461
	6	1.0000	1.0000	1.0000	0.9999	0.9997	0.9987	0.9957	0.9917	0.9750	0.9102
	7	1.0000	1.0000	1.0000	1.0000	1.0000	0.9999	0.9996	0.9990	0.9962	0.9805
	8	1.0000	1.0000	1.0000	1.0000	1.0000	1.0000	1.0000	0.9999	0.9997	0.9980

Binomialverteilung: Verteilungsfunktion $F_{Bi}(x;p,n)$: Fortsetzung

		\multicolumn{10}{c}{Erfolgswahrscheinlichkeit p}
n	x	0.02	0.05	0.10	$\frac{1}{6}$	0.20	0.25	0.30	$\frac{1}{3}$	0.40	0.50
10	0	0.8171	0.5987	0.3487	0.1615	0.1074	0.0563	0.0282	0.0173	0.0060	0.0010
	1	0.9838	0.9139	0.7361	0.4845	0.3758	0.2440	0.1493	0.1040	0.0464	0.0107
	2	0.9991	0.9885	0.9298	0.7752	0.6778	0.5256	0.3828	0.2991	0.1673	0.0547
	3	1.0000	0.9990	0.9872	0.9303	0.8791	0.7759	0.6496	0.5593	0.3823	0.1719
	4	1.0000	0.9999	0.9984	0.9845	0.9672	0.9219	0.8497	0.7869	0.6331	0.3770
	5	1.0000	1.0000	0.9999	0.9976	0.9936	0.9803	0.9527	0.9234	0.8338	0.6230
	6	1.0000	1.0000	1.0000	0.9997	0.9991	0.9965	0.9894	0.9803	0.9452	0.8281
	7	1.0000	1.0000	1.0000	1.0000	0.9999	0.9996	0.9984	0.9966	0.9877	0.9453
	8	1.0000	1.0000	1.0000	1.0000	1.0000	1.0000	0.9999	0.9996	0.9983	0.9893
	9	1.0000	1.0000	1.0000	1.0000	1.0000	1.0000	1.0000	1.0000	0.9999	0.9990
11	0	0.8007	0.5688	0.3138	0.1346	0.0859	0.0422	0.0198	0.0116	0.0036	0.0005
	1	0.9805	0.8981	0.6974	0.4307	0.3221	0.1971	0.1130	0.0751	0.0302	0.0059
	2	0.9988	0.9848	0.9104	0.7268	0.6174	0.4552	0.3127	0.2341	0.1189	0.0327
	3	1.0000	0.9984	0.9815	0.9044	0.8389	0.7133	0.5696	0.4726	0.2963	0.1133
	4	1.0000	0.9999	0.9972	0.9755	0.9496	0.8854	0.7897	0.7110	0.5328	0.2744
	5	1.0000	1.0000	0.9997	0.9954	0.9883	0.9657	0.9218	0.8779	0.7535	0.5000
	6	1.0000	1.0000	1.0000	0.9994	0.9980	0.9924	0.9784	0.9614	0.9006	0.7256
	7	1.0000	1.0000	1.0000	0.9999	0.9998	0.9988	0.9957	0.9912	0.9707	0.8867
	8	1.0000	1.0000	1.0000	1.0000	1.0000	0.9999	0.9994	0.9986	0.9941	0.9673
	9	1.0000	1.0000	1.0000	1.0000	1.0000	1.0000	1.0000	0.9999	0.9993	0.9941
	10	1.0000	1.0000	1.0000	1.0000	1.0000	1.0000	1.0000	1.0000	1.0000	0.9995
12	0	0.7847	0.5404	0.2824	0.1122	0.0687	0.0317	0.0138	0.0077	0.0022	0.0002
	1	0.9769	0.8816	0.6590	0.3813	0.2749	0.1584	0.0850	0.0540	0.0196	0.0032
	2	0.9985	0.9804	0.8891	0.6774	0.5583	0.3907	0.2528	0.1811	0.0834	0.0193
	3	0.9999	0.9978	0.9744	0.8748	0.7946	0.6488	0.4925	0.3931	0.2253	0.0730
	4	1.0000	0.9998	0.9957	0.9636	0.9274	0.8424	0.7237	0.6315	0.4382	0.1938
	5	1.0000	1.0000	0.9995	0.9921	0.9806	0.9456	0.8822	0.8223	0.6652	0.3872
	6	1.0000	1.0000	0.9999	0.9987	0.9961	0.9857	0.9614	0.9336	0.8418	0.6128
	7	1.0000	1.0000	1.0000	0.9998	0.9994	0.9972	0.9905	0.9812	0.9427	0.8062
	8	1.0000	1.0000	1.0000	1.0000	0.9999	0.9996	0.9983	0.9961	0.9847	0.9270
	9	1.0000	1.0000	1.0000	1.0000	1.0000	1.0000	0.9998	0.9995	0.9972	0.9807
	10	1.0000	1.0000	1.0000	1.0000	1.0000	1.0000	1.0000	1.0000	0.9997	0.9968
	11	1.0000	1.0000	1.0000	1.0000	1.0000	1.0000	1.0000	1.0000	1.0000	0.9998
13	0	0.7690	0.5133	0.2542	0.0935	0.0550	0.0238	0.0097	0.0051	0.0013	0.0001
	1	0.9730	0.8646	0.6213	0.3365	0.2336	0.1267	0.0637	0.0385	0.0126	0.0017
	2	0.9980	0.9755	0.8661	0.6281	0.5017	0.3326	0.2025	0.1387	0.0579	0.0112
	3	0.9999	0.9969	0.9658	0.8419	0.7473	0.5843	0.4206	0.3224	0.1686	0.0461
	4	1.0000	0.9997	0.9935	0.9488	0.9009	0.7940	0.6543	0.5520	0.3530	0.1334
	5	1.0000	1.0000	0.9991	0.9873	0.9700	0.9198	0.8346	0.7587	0.5744	0.2905
	6	1.0000	1.0000	0.9999	0.9976	0.9930	0.9757	0.9376	0.8965	0.7712	0.5000
	7	1.0000	1.0000	1.0000	0.9997	0.9988	0.9944	0.9818	0.9653	0.9023	0.7095
	8	1.0000	1.0000	1.0000	1.0000	0.9998	0.9990	0.9960	0.9912	0.9679	0.8666
	9	1.0000	1.0000	1.0000	1.0000	1.0000	0.9999	0.9993	0.9984	0.9922	0.9539
	10	1.0000	1.0000	1.0000	1.0000	1.0000	1.0000	0.9999	0.9998	0.9987	0.9888
	11	1.0000	1.0000	1.0000	1.0000	1.0000	1.0000	1.0000	1.0000	0.9999	0.9983
	12	1.0000	1.0000	1.0000	1.0000	1.0000	1.0000	1.0000	1.0000	1.0000	0.9999

Binomialverteilung: Verteilungsfunktion $F_{Bi}(x;p,n)$: Fortsetzung

n	x	\multicolumn{10}{c}{Erfolgswahrscheinlichkeit p}									
		0.02	0.05	0.10	$\frac{1}{6}$	0.20	0.25	0.30	$\frac{1}{3}$	0.40	0.50
14	0	0.7536	0.4877	0.2288	0.0779	0.0440	0.0178	0.0068	0.0034	0.0008	0.0001
	1	0.9690	0.8470	0.5846	0.2960	0.1979	0.1010	0.0475	0.0274	0.0081	0.0009
	2	0.9975	0.9699	0.8416	0.5795	0.4481	0.2811	0.1608	0.1053	0.0398	0.0065
	3	0.9999	0.9958	0.9559	0.8063	0.6982	0.5213	0.3552	0.2612	0.1243	0.0287
	4	1.0000	0.9996	0.9908	0.9310	0.8702	0.7415	0.5842	0.4755	0.2793	0.0898
	5	1.0000	1.0000	0.9985	0.9809	0.9561	0.8883	0.7805	0.6898	0.4859	0.2120
	6	1.0000	1.0000	0.9998	0.9959	0.9884	0.9617	0.9067	0.8505	0.6925	0.3953
	7	1.0000	1.0000	1.0000	0.9993	0.9976	0.9897	0.9685	0.9424	0.8499	0.6047
	8	1.0000	1.0000	1.0000	0.9999	0.9996	0.9978	0.9917	0.9826	0.9417	0.7880
	9	1.0000	1.0000	1.0000	1.0000	1.0000	0.9997	0.9983	0.9960	0.9825	0.9102
	10	1.0000	1.0000	1.0000	1.0000	1.0000	1.0000	0.9998	0.9993	0.9961	0.9713
	11	1.0000	1.0000	1.0000	1.0000	1.0000	1.0000	1.0000	0.9999	0.9994	0.9935
	12	1.0000	1.0000	1.0000	1.0000	1.0000	1.0000	1.0000	1.0000	0.9999	0.9991
	13	1.0000	1.0000	1.0000	1.0000	1.0000	1.0000	1.0000	1.0000	1.0000	0.9999
15	0	0.7386	0.4633	0.2059	0.0649	0.0352	0.0134	0.0047	0.0023	0.0005	0.0000
	1	0.9647	0.8290	0.5490	0.2596	0.1671	0.0802	0.0353	0.0194	0.0052	0.0005
	2	0.9970	0.9638	0.8159	0.5322	0.3980	0.2361	0.1268	0.0794	0.0271	0.0037
	3	0.9998	0.9945	0.9444	0.7685	0.6482	0.4613	0.2969	0.2092	0.0905	0.0176
	4	1.0000	0.9994	0.9873	0.9102	0.8358	0.6865	0.5155	0.4041	0.2173	0.0592
	5	1.0000	0.9999	0.9978	0.9726	0.9389	0.8516	0.7216	0.6184	0.4032	0.1509
	6	1.0000	1.0000	0.9997	0.9934	0.9819	0.9434	0.8689	0.7970	0.6098	0.3036
	7	1.0000	1.0000	1.0000	0.9987	0.9958	0.9827	0.9500	0.9118	0.7869	0.5000
	8	1.0000	1.0000	1.0000	0.9998	0.9992	0.9958	0.9848	0.9692	0.9050	0.6964
	9	1.0000	1.0000	1.0000	1.0000	0.9999	0.9992	0.9963	0.9915	0.9662	0.8491
	10	1.0000	1.0000	1.0000	1.0000	1.0000	0.9999	0.9993	0.9982	0.9907	0.9408
	11	1.0000	1.0000	1.0000	1.0000	1.0000	1.0000	0.9999	0.9997	0.9981	0.9824
	12	1.0000	1.0000	1.0000	1.0000	1.0000	1.0000	1.0000	1.0000	0.9997	0.9963
	13	1.0000	1.0000	1.0000	1.0000	1.0000	1.0000	1.0000	1.0000	1.0000	0.9995
	14	1.0000	1.0000	1.0000	1.0000	1.0000	1.0000	1.0000	1.0000	1.0000	1.0000
20	0	0.6676	0.3585	0.1216	0.0261	0.0115	0.0032	0.0008	0.0003	0.0000	0.0000
	1	0.9401	0.7358	0.3917	0.1304	0.0692	0.0243	0.0076	0.0033	0.0005	0.0000
	2	0.9929	0.9245	0.6769	0.3287	0.2061	0.0913	0.0355	0.0176	0.0036	0.0002
	3	0.9994	0.9841	0.8670	0.5665	0.4114	0.2252	0.1071	0.0604	0.0160	0.0013
	4	1.0000	0.9974	0.9568	0.7687	0.6296	0.4148	0.2375	0.1515	0.0510	0.0059
	5	1.0000	0.9997	0.9887	0.8982	0.8042	0.6172	0.4164	0.2972	0.1256	0.0207
	6	1.0000	1.0000	0.9976	0.9629	0.9133	0.7858	0.6080	0.4793	0.2500	0.0577
	7	1.0000	1.0000	0.9996	0.9887	0.9679	0.8982	0.7723	0.6615	0.4159	0.1316
	8	1.0000	1.0000	0.9999	0.9972	0.9900	0.9591	0.8867	0.8095	0.5956	0.2517
	9	1.0000	1.0000	1.0000	0.9994	0.9974	0.9861	0.9520	0.9081	0.7553	0.4119
	10	1.0000	1.0000	1.0000	0.9999	0.9994	0.9961	0.9829	0.9624	0.8725	0.5881
	11	1.0000	1.0000	1.0000	1.0000	0.9999	0.9991	0.9949	0.9870	0.9435	0.7483
	12	1.0000	1.0000	1.0000	1.0000	1.0000	0.9998	0.9987	0.9963	0.9790	0.8684
	13	1.0000	1.0000	1.0000	1.0000	1.0000	1.0000	0.9997	0.9991	0.9935	0.9423
	14	1.0000	1.0000	1.0000	1.0000	1.0000	1.0000	1.0000	0.9998	0.9984	0.9793
	15	1.0000	1.0000	1.0000	1.0000	1.0000	1.0000	1.0000	1.0000	0.9997	0.9941
	16	1.0000	1.0000	1.0000	1.0000	1.0000	1.0000	1.0000	1.0000	1.0000	0.9987
	17	1.0000	1.0000	1.0000	1.0000	1.0000	1.0000	1.0000	1.0000	1.0000	0.9998
	18	1.0000	1.0000	1.0000	1.0000	1.0000	1.0000	1.0000	1.0000	1.0000	1.0000
	19	1.0000	1.0000	1.0000	1.0000	1.0000	1.0000	1.0000	1.0000	1.0000	1.0000

5.3 Standardnormalverteilung: Verteilungsfunktion $F_{\mathcal{N}}(q;0,1) = \Phi(z)$

- R Code: pnorm(z)
- Für negative Werte z: $\Phi(z) = 1 - \Phi(-z)$
- Allgemeine Normalverteilung: $F_{\mathcal{N}}(x;\mu,\sigma^2) = \Phi\left(\frac{x-\mu}{\sigma}\right)$

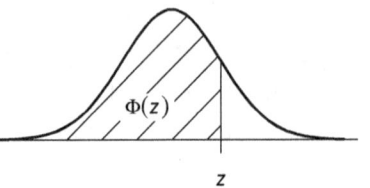

		Zweite Nachkommastelle von z								
		0.00	0.01	0.02	0.03	0.04	0.05	0.06	0.07	0.08	0.09
Erste Vor- und Nachkommastelle von z	0.0	0.5000	0.5040	0.5080	0.5120	0.5160	0.5199	0.5239	0.5279	0.5319	0.5359
	0.1	0.5398	0.5438	0.5478	0.5517	0.5557	0.5596	0.5636	0.5675	0.5714	0.5753
	0.2	0.5793	0.5832	0.5871	0.5910	0.5948	0.5987	0.6026	0.6064	0.6103	0.6141
	0.3	0.6179	0.6217	0.6255	0.6293	0.6331	0.6368	0.6406	0.6443	0.6480	0.6517
	0.4	0.6554	0.6591	0.6628	0.6664	0.6700	0.6736	0.6772	0.6808	0.6844	0.6879
	0.5	0.6915	0.6950	0.6985	0.7019	0.7054	0.7088	0.7123	0.7157	0.7190	0.7224
	0.6	0.7257	0.7291	0.7324	0.7357	0.7389	0.7422	0.7454	0.7486	0.7517	0.7549
	0.7	0.7580	0.7611	0.7642	0.7673	0.7704	0.7734	0.7764	0.7794	0.7823	0.7852
	0.8	0.7881	0.7910	0.7939	0.7967	0.7995	0.8023	0.8051	0.8078	0.8106	0.8133
	0.9	0.8159	0.8186	0.8212	0.8238	0.8264	0.8289	0.8315	0.8340	0.8365	0.8389
	1.0	0.8413	0.8438	0.8461	0.8485	0.8508	0.8531	0.8554	0.8577	0.8599	0.8621
	1.1	0.8643	0.8665	0.8686	0.8708	0.8729	0.8749	0.8770	0.8790	0.8810	0.8830
	1.2	0.8849	0.8869	0.8888	0.8907	0.8925	0.8944	0.8962	0.8980	0.8997	0.9015
	1.3	0.9032	0.9049	0.9066	0.9082	0.9099	0.9115	0.9131	0.9147	0.9162	0.9177
	1.4	0.9192	0.9207	0.9222	0.9236	0.9251	0.9265	0.9279	0.9292	0.9306	0.9319
	1.5	0.9332	0.9345	0.9357	0.9370	0.9382	0.9394	0.9406	0.9418	0.9429	0.9441
	1.6	0.9452	0.9463	0.9474	0.9484	0.9495	0.9505	0.9515	0.9525	0.9535	0.9545
	1.7	0.9554	0.9564	0.9573	0.9582	0.9591	0.9599	0.9608	0.9616	0.9625	0.9633
	1.8	0.9641	0.9649	0.9656	0.9664	0.9671	0.9678	0.9686	0.9693	0.9699	0.9706
	1.9	0.9713	0.9719	0.9726	0.9732	0.9738	0.9744	0.9750	0.9756	0.9761	0.9767
	2.0	0.9772	0.9778	0.9783	0.9788	0.9793	0.9798	0.9803	0.9808	0.9812	0.9817
	2.1	0.9821	0.9826	0.9830	0.9834	0.9838	0.9842	0.9846	0.9850	0.9854	0.9857
	2.2	0.9861	0.9864	0.9868	0.9871	0.9875	0.9878	0.9881	0.9884	0.9887	0.9890
	2.3	0.9893	0.9896	0.9898	0.9901	0.9904	0.9906	0.9909	0.9911	0.9913	0.9916
	2.4	0.9918	0.9920	0.9922	0.9925	0.9927	0.9929	0.9931	0.9932	0.9934	0.9936
	2.5	0.9938	0.9940	0.9941	0.9943	0.9945	0.9946	0.9948	0.9949	0.9951	0.9952
	2.6	0.9953	0.9955	0.9956	0.9957	0.9959	0.9960	0.9961	0.9962	0.9963	0.9964
	2.7	0.9965	0.9966	0.9967	0.9968	0.9969	0.9970	0.9971	0.9972	0.9973	0.9974
	2.8	0.9974	0.9975	0.9976	0.9977	0.9977	0.9978	0.9979	0.9979	0.9980	0.9981
	2.9	0.9981	0.9982	0.9982	0.9983	0.9984	0.9984	0.9985	0.9985	0.9986	0.9986
	3.0	0.9987	0.9987	0.9987	0.9988	0.9988	0.9989	0.9989	0.9989	0.9990	0.9990
	3.1	0.9990	0.9991	0.9991	0.9991	0.9992	0.9992	0.9992	0.9992	0.9993	0.9993
	3.2	0.9993	0.9993	0.9994	0.9994	0.9994	0.9994	0.9994	0.9995	0.9995	0.9995
	3.3	0.9995	0.9995	0.9995	0.9996	0.9996	0.9996	0.9996	0.9996	0.9996	0.9997
	3.4	0.9997	0.9997	0.9997	0.9997	0.9997	0.9997	0.9997	0.9997	0.9997	0.9998
	3.5	0.9998	0.9998	0.9998	0.9998	0.9998	0.9998	0.9998	0.9998	0.9998	0.9998
	3.6	0.9998	0.9998	0.9999	0.9999	0.9999	0.9999	0.9999	0.9999	0.9999	0.9999
	3.7	0.9999	0.9999	0.9999	0.9999	0.9999	0.9999	0.9999	0.9999	0.9999	0.9999
	3.8	0.9999	0.9999	0.9999	0.9999	0.9999	0.9999	0.9999	0.9999	0.9999	0.9999
	3.9	1.0000	1.0000	1.0000	1.0000	1.0000	1.0000	1.0000	1.0000	1.0000	1.0000

5.4 Standardnormalverteilung: Quantilsfunktion $Q_{\mathcal{N}}(q; 0, 1) = \Phi^{-1}(q)$

		\multicolumn{10}{c}{Dritte Nachkommastelle von q}
		0.000	0.001	0.002	0.003	0.004	0.005	0.006	0.007	0.008	0.009
	0.50	0.0000	0.0025	0.0050	0.0075	0.0100	0.0125	0.0150	0.0175	0.0201	0.0226
	0.51	0.0251	0.0276	0.0301	0.0326	0.0351	0.0376	0.0401	0.0426	0.0451	0.0476
	0.52	0.0502	0.0527	0.0552	0.0577	0.0602	0.0627	0.0652	0.0677	0.0702	0.0728
	0.53	0.0753	0.0778	0.0803	0.0828	0.0853	0.0878	0.0904	0.0929	0.0954	0.0979
	0.54	0.1004	0.1030	0.1055	0.1080	0.1105	0.1130	0.1156	0.1181	0.1206	0.1231
	0.55	0.1257	0.1282	0.1307	0.1332	0.1358	0.1383	0.1408	0.1434	0.1459	0.1484
	0.56	0.1510	0.1535	0.1560	0.1586	0.1611	0.1637	0.1662	0.1687	0.1713	0.1738
	0.57	0.1764	0.1789	0.1815	0.1840	0.1866	0.1891	0.1917	0.1942	0.1968	0.1993
	0.58	0.2019	0.2045	0.2070	0.2096	0.2121	0.2147	0.2173	0.2198	0.2224	0.2250
	0.59	0.2275	0.2301	0.2327	0.2353	0.2378	0.2404	0.2430	0.2456	0.2482	0.2508
	0.60	0.2533	0.2559	0.2585	0.2611	0.2637	0.2663	0.2689	0.2715	0.2741	0.2767
	0.61	0.2793	0.2819	0.2845	0.2871	0.2898	0.2924	0.2950	0.2976	0.3002	0.3029
	0.62	0.3055	0.3081	0.3107	0.3134	0.3160	0.3186	0.3213	0.3239	0.3266	0.3292
	0.63	0.3319	0.3345	0.3372	0.3398	0.3425	0.3451	0.3478	0.3505	0.3531	0.3558
	0.64	0.3585	0.3611	0.3638	0.3665	0.3692	0.3719	0.3745	0.3772	0.3799	0.3826
	0.65	0.3853	0.3880	0.3907	0.3934	0.3961	0.3989	0.4016	0.4043	0.4070	0.4097
	0.66	0.4125	0.4152	0.4179	0.4207	0.4234	0.4261	0.4289	0.4316	0.4344	0.4372
Erste und zweite Nachkommastelle von q	0.67	0.4399	0.4427	0.4454	0.4482	0.4510	0.4538	0.4565	0.4593	0.4621	0.4649
	0.68	0.4677	0.4705	0.4733	0.4761	0.4789	0.4817	0.4845	0.4874	0.4902	0.4930
	0.69	0.4959	0.4987	0.5015	0.5044	0.5072	0.5101	0.5129	0.5158	0.5187	0.5215
	0.70	0.5244	0.5273	0.5302	0.5330	0.5359	0.5388	0.5417	0.5446	0.5476	0.5505
	0.71	0.5534	0.5563	0.5592	0.5622	0.5651	0.5681	0.5710	0.5740	0.5769	0.5799
	0.72	0.5828	0.5858	0.5888	0.5918	0.5948	0.5978	0.6008	0.6038	0.6068	0.6098
	0.73	0.6128	0.6158	0.6189	0.6219	0.6250	0.6280	0.6311	0.6341	0.6372	0.6403
	0.74	0.6433	0.6464	0.6495	0.6526	0.6557	0.6588	0.6620	0.6651	0.6682	0.6713
	0.75	0.6745	0.6776	0.6808	0.6840	0.6871	0.6903	0.6935	0.6967	0.6999	0.7031
	0.76	0.7063	0.7095	0.7128	0.7160	0.7192	0.7225	0.7257	0.7290	0.7323	0.7356
	0.77	0.7388	0.7421	0.7454	0.7488	0.7521	0.7554	0.7588	0.7621	0.7655	0.7688
	0.78	0.7722	0.7756	0.7790	0.7824	0.7858	0.7892	0.7926	0.7961	0.7995	0.8030
	0.79	0.8064	0.8099	0.8134	0.8169	0.8204	0.8239	0.8274	0.8310	0.8345	0.8381
	0.80	0.8416	0.8452	0.8488	0.8524	0.8560	0.8596	0.8633	0.8669	0.8705	0.8742
	0.81	0.8779	0.8816	0.8853	0.8890	0.8927	0.8965	0.9002	0.9040	0.9078	0.9116
	0.82	0.9154	0.9192	0.9230	0.9269	0.9307	0.9346	0.9385	0.9424	0.9463	0.9502
	0.83	0.9542	0.9581	0.9621	0.9661	0.9701	0.9741	0.9782	0.9822	0.9863	0.9904
	0.84	0.9945	0.9986	1.0027	1.0069	1.0110	1.0152	1.0194	1.0237	1.0279	1.0322
	0.85	1.0364	1.0407	1.0450	1.0494	1.0537	1.0581	1.0625	1.0669	1.0714	1.0758
	0.86	1.0803	1.0848	1.0893	1.0939	1.0985	1.1031	1.1077	1.1123	1.1170	1.1217
	0.87	1.1264	1.1311	1.1359	1.1407	1.1455	1.1503	1.1552	1.1601	1.1650	1.1700
	0.88	1.1750	1.1800	1.1850	1.1901	1.1952	1.2004	1.2055	1.2107	1.2160	1.2212
	0.89	1.2265	1.2319	1.2372	1.2426	1.2481	1.2536	1.2591	1.2646	1.2702	1.2759
	0.90	1.2816	1.2873	1.2930	1.2988	1.3047	1.3106	1.3165	1.3225	1.3285	1.3346
	0.91	1.3408	1.3469	1.3532	1.3595	1.3658	1.3722	1.3787	1.3852	1.3917	1.3984
	0.92	1.4051	1.4118	1.4187	1.4255	1.4325	1.4395	1.4466	1.4538	1.4611	1.4684
	0.93	1.4758	1.4833	1.4909	1.4985	1.5063	1.5141	1.5220	1.5301	1.5382	1.5464
	0.94	1.5548	1.5632	1.5718	1.5805	1.5893	1.5982	1.6072	1.6164	1.6258	1.6352
	0.95	1.6449	1.6546	1.6646	1.6747	1.6849	1.6954	1.7060	1.7169	1.7279	1.7392
	0.96	1.7507	1.7624	1.7744	1.7866	1.7991	1.8119	1.8250	1.8384	1.8522	1.8663
	0.97	1.8808	1.8957	1.9110	1.9268	1.9431	1.9600	1.9774	1.9954	2.0141	2.0335
	0.98	2.0537	2.0749	2.0969	2.1201	2.1444	2.1701	2.1973	2.2262	2.2571	2.2904
	0.99	2.3263	2.3656	2.4089	2.4573	2.5121	2.5758	2.6521	2.7478	2.8782	3.0902

5.5 χ^2-Verteilung: Quantilsfunktion $Q_{\chi^2}(q;n)$

- R Code: `qchisq(q,n)`

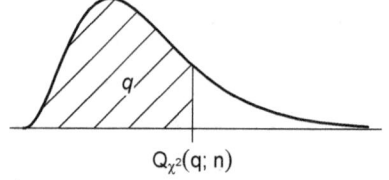

		\multicolumn{9}{c}{Quantil q}								
		0.010	0.025	0.050	0.100	0.900	0.950	0.975	0.990	0.995
	1	0.000	0.001	0.004	0.016	2.706	3.841	5.024	6.635	7.879
	2	0.020	0.051	0.103	0.211	4.605	5.991	7.378	9.210	10.597
	3	0.115	0.216	0.352	0.584	6.251	7.815	9.348	11.345	12.838
	4	0.297	0.484	0.711	1.064	7.779	9.488	11.143	13.277	14.860
	5	0.554	0.831	1.145	1.610	9.236	11.070	12.833	15.086	16.750
	6	0.872	1.237	1.635	2.204	10.645	12.592	14.449	16.812	18.548
	7	1.239	1.690	2.167	2.833	12.017	14.067	16.013	18.475	20.278
	8	1.646	2.180	2.733	3.490	13.362	15.507	17.535	20.090	21.955
	9	2.088	2.700	3.325	4.168	14.684	16.919	19.023	21.666	23.589
	10	2.558	3.247	3.940	4.865	15.987	18.307	20.483	23.209	25.188
	11	3.053	3.816	4.575	5.578	17.275	19.675	21.920	24.725	26.757
	12	3.571	4.404	5.226	6.304	18.549	21.026	23.337	26.217	28.300
	13	4.107	5.009	5.892	7.042	19.812	22.362	24.736	27.688	29.819
	14	4.660	5.629	6.571	7.790	21.064	23.685	26.119	29.141	31.319
	15	5.229	6.262	7.261	8.547	22.307	24.996	27.488	30.578	32.801
	16	5.812	6.908	7.962	9.312	23.542	26.296	28.845	32.000	34.267
	17	6.408	7.564	8.672	10.085	24.769	27.587	30.191	33.409	35.718
	18	7.015	8.231	9.390	10.865	25.989	28.869	31.526	34.805	37.156
Freiheitsgrade n	19	7.633	8.907	10.117	11.651	27.204	30.144	32.852	36.191	38.582
	20	8.260	9.591	10.851	12.443	28.412	31.410	34.170	37.566	39.997
	21	8.897	10.283	11.591	13.240	29.615	32.671	35.479	38.932	41.401
	22	9.542	10.982	12.338	14.041	30.813	33.924	36.781	40.289	42.796
	23	10.196	11.689	13.091	14.848	32.007	35.172	38.076	41.638	44.181
	24	10.856	12.401	13.848	15.659	33.196	36.415	39.364	42.980	45.559
	25	11.524	13.120	14.611	16.473	34.382	37.652	40.646	44.314	46.928
	26	12.198	13.844	15.379	17.292	35.563	38.885	41.923	45.642	48.290
	27	12.879	14.573	16.151	18.114	36.741	40.113	43.195	46.963	49.645
	28	13.565	15.308	16.928	18.939	37.916	41.337	44.461	48.278	50.993
	29	14.256	16.047	17.708	19.768	39.087	42.557	45.722	49.588	52.336
	30	14.953	16.791	18.493	20.599	40.256	43.773	46.979	50.892	53.672
	31	15.655	17.539	19.281	21.434	41.422	44.985	48.232	52.191	55.003
	32	16.362	18.291	20.072	22.271	42.585	46.194	49.480	53.486	56.328
	33	17.074	19.047	20.867	23.110	43.745	47.400	50.725	54.776	57.648
	34	17.789	19.806	21.664	23.952	44.903	48.602	51.966	56.061	58.964
	35	18.509	20.569	22.465	24.797	46.059	49.802	53.203	57.342	60.275
	36	19.233	21.336	23.269	25.643	47.212	50.998	54.437	58.619	61.581
	37	19.960	22.106	24.075	26.492	48.363	52.192	55.668	59.893	62.883
	38	20.691	22.878	24.884	27.343	49.513	53.384	56.896	61.162	64.181
	39	21.426	23.654	25.695	28.196	50.660	54.572	58.120	62.428	65.476
	40	22.164	24.433	26.509	29.051	51.805	55.758	59.342	63.691	66.766

χ^2-Verteilung: Quantilsfunktion $Q_{\chi^2}(q;n)$ (Fortsetzung)

		\multicolumn{9}{c}{Quantil q}
		0.010	0.025	0.050	0.100	0.900	0.950	0.975	0.990	0.995
Freiheitsgrade n	41	22.906	25.215	27.326	29.907	52.949	56.942	60.561	64.950	68.053
	42	23.650	25.999	28.144	30.765	54.090	58.124	61.777	66.206	69.336
	43	24.398	26.785	28.965	31.625	55.230	59.304	62.990	67.459	70.616
	44	25.148	27.575	29.787	32.487	56.369	60.481	64.201	68.710	71.893
	45	25.901	28.366	30.612	33.350	57.505	61.656	65.410	69.957	73.166
	46	26.657	29.160	31.439	34.215	58.641	62.830	66.617	71.201	74.437
	47	27.416	29.956	32.268	35.081	59.774	64.001	67.821	72.443	75.704
	48	28.177	30.755	33.098	35.949	60.907	65.171	69.023	73.683	76.969
	49	28.941	31.555	33.930	36.818	62.038	66.339	70.222	74.919	78.231
	50	29.707	32.357	34.764	37.689	63.167	67.505	71.420	76.154	79.490
	55	33.570	36.398	38.958	42.060	68.796	73.311	77.380	82.292	85.749
	60	37.485	40.482	43.188	46.459	74.397	79.082	83.298	88.379	91.952
	65	41.444	44.603	47.450	50.883	79.973	84.821	89.177	94.422	98.105
	70	45.442	48.758	51.739	55.329	85.527	90.531	95.023	100.425	104.215
	75	49.475	52.942	56.054	59.795	91.061	96.217	100.839	106.393	110.286
	80	53.540	57.153	60.391	64.278	96.578	101.879	106.629	112.329	116.321
	85	57.634	61.389	64.749	68.777	102.079	107.522	112.393	118.236	122.325
	90	61.754	65.647	69.126	73.291	107.565	113.145	118.136	124.116	128.299
	95	65.898	69.925	73.520	77.818	113.038	118.752	123.858	129.973	134.247
	100	70.065	74.222	77.929	82.358	118.498	124.342	129.561	135.807	140.169
	105	74.252	78.536	82.354	86.909	123.947	129.918	135.247	141.620	146.070
	110	78.458	82.867	86.792	91.471	129.385	135.480	140.917	147.414	151.948
	115	82.682	87.213	91.242	96.043	134.813	141.030	146.571	153.191	157.808
	120	86.923	91.573	95.705	100.624	140.233	146.567	152.211	158.950	163.648
	125	91.180	95.946	100.178	105.213	145.643	152.094	157.839	164.694	169.471
	130	95.451	100.331	104.662	109.811	151.045	157.610	163.453	170.423	175.278
	135	99.736	104.729	109.156	114.417	156.440	163.116	169.056	176.138	181.070
	140	104.034	109.137	113.659	119.029	161.827	168.613	174.648	181.840	186.847
	145	108.345	113.556	118.171	123.649	167.207	174.101	180.229	187.530	192.610
	150	112.668	117.985	122.692	128.275	172.581	179.581	185.800	193.208	198.360
	155	117.001	122.423	127.220	132.907	177.949	185.052	191.362	198.874	204.098
	160	121.346	126.870	131.756	137.546	183.311	190.516	196.915	204.530	209.824
	165	125.700	131.326	136.299	142.190	188.667	195.973	202.459	210.176	215.539
	170	130.064	135.790	140.849	146.839	194.017	201.423	207.995	215.812	221.242
	175	134.438	140.262	145.406	151.493	199.363	206.867	213.524	221.438	226.936
	180	138.820	144.741	149.969	156.153	204.704	212.304	219.044	227.056	232.620
	185	143.211	149.228	154.538	160.817	210.040	217.735	224.558	232.665	238.294
	190	147.610	153.721	159.113	165.485	215.371	223.160	230.064	238.266	243.959
	195	152.017	158.221	163.693	170.158	220.698	228.580	235.564	243.860	249.616
	200	156.432	162.728	168.279	174.835	226.021	233.994	241.058	249.445	255.264
	250	200.939	208.098	214.392	221.806	279.050	287.882	295.689	304.940	311.346
	300	245.972	253.912	260.878	269.068	331.789	341.395	349.874	359.906	366.844
	350	291.406	300.064	307.648	316.550	384.306	394.626	403.723	414.474	421.900
	400	337.155	346.482	354.641	364.207	436.649	447.632	457.305	468.724	476.606
	450	383.163	393.118	401.817	412.007	488.849	500.456	510.670	522.717	531.026
	500	429.388	439.936	449.147	459.926	540.930	553.127	563.852	576.493	585.207

5.6 t-Verteilung: Quantilsfunktion $Q_t(q;n)$

- Symmetrie: Für Werte $q < 0.5$: $Q_t(q;n) = -Q_t(1-q;n)$
- R Code: qt(q,n)

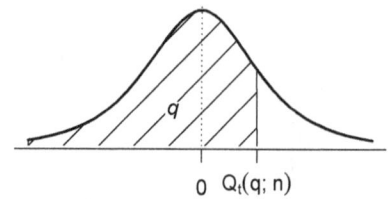

		Quantil q									
		0.500	0.600	0.700	0.800	0.850	0.900	0.950	0.975	0.990	0.995	0.999
Freiheitsgrade n	1	0.000	0.325	0.727	1.376	1.963	3.078	6.314	12.706	31.821	63.657	318.309
	2	0.000	0.289	0.617	1.061	1.386	1.886	2.920	4.303	6.965	9.925	22.327
	3	0.000	0.277	0.584	0.978	1.250	1.638	2.353	3.182	4.541	5.841	10.215
	4	0.000	0.271	0.569	0.941	1.190	1.533	2.132	2.776	3.747	4.604	7.173
	5	0.000	0.267	0.559	0.920	1.156	1.476	2.015	2.571	3.365	4.032	5.893
	6	0.000	0.265	0.553	0.906	1.134	1.440	1.943	2.447	3.143	3.707	5.208
	7	0.000	0.263	0.549	0.896	1.119	1.415	1.895	2.365	2.998	3.499	4.785
	8	0.000	0.262	0.546	0.889	1.108	1.397	1.860	2.306	2.896	3.355	4.501
	9	0.000	0.261	0.543	0.883	1.100	1.383	1.833	2.262	2.821	3.250	4.297
	10	0.000	0.260	0.542	0.879	1.093	1.372	1.812	2.228	2.764	3.169	4.144
	11	0.000	0.260	0.540	0.876	1.088	1.363	1.796	2.201	2.718	3.106	4.025
	12	0.000	0.259	0.539	0.873	1.083	1.356	1.782	2.179	2.681	3.055	3.930
	13	0.000	0.259	0.538	0.870	1.079	1.350	1.771	2.160	2.650	3.012	3.852
	14	0.000	0.258	0.537	0.868	1.076	1.345	1.761	2.145	2.624	2.977	3.787
	15	0.000	0.258	0.536	0.866	1.074	1.341	1.753	2.131	2.602	2.947	3.733
	16	0.000	0.258	0.535	0.865	1.071	1.337	1.746	2.120	2.583	2.921	3.686
	17	0.000	0.257	0.534	0.863	1.069	1.333	1.740	2.110	2.567	2.898	3.646
	18	0.000	0.257	0.534	0.862	1.067	1.330	1.734	2.101	2.552	2.878	3.610
	19	0.000	0.257	0.533	0.861	1.066	1.328	1.729	2.093	2.539	2.861	3.579
	20	0.000	0.257	0.533	0.860	1.064	1.325	1.725	2.086	2.528	2.845	3.552
	21	0.000	0.257	0.532	0.859	1.063	1.323	1.721	2.080	2.518	2.831	3.527
	22	0.000	0.256	0.532	0.858	1.061	1.321	1.717	2.074	2.508	2.819	3.505
	23	0.000	0.256	0.532	0.858	1.060	1.319	1.714	2.069	2.500	2.807	3.485
	24	0.000	0.256	0.531	0.857	1.059	1.318	1.711	2.064	2.492	2.797	3.467
	25	0.000	0.256	0.531	0.856	1.058	1.316	1.708	2.060	2.485	2.787	3.450
	26	0.000	0.256	0.531	0.856	1.058	1.315	1.706	2.056	2.479	2.779	3.435
	27	0.000	0.256	0.531	0.855	1.057	1.314	1.703	2.052	2.473	2.771	3.421
	28	0.000	0.256	0.530	0.855	1.056	1.313	1.701	2.048	2.467	2.763	3.408
	29	0.000	0.256	0.530	0.854	1.055	1.311	1.699	2.045	2.462	2.756	3.396
	30	0.000	0.256	0.530	0.854	1.055	1.310	1.697	2.042	2.457	2.750	3.385
	31	0.000	0.256	0.530	0.853	1.054	1.309	1.696	2.040	2.453	2.744	3.375
	32	0.000	0.255	0.530	0.853	1.054	1.309	1.694	2.037	2.449	2.738	3.365
	33	0.000	0.255	0.530	0.853	1.053	1.308	1.692	2.035	2.445	2.733	3.356
	34	0.000	0.255	0.529	0.852	1.052	1.307	1.691	2.032	2.441	2.728	3.348
	35	0.000	0.255	0.529	0.852	1.052	1.306	1.690	2.030	2.438	2.724	3.340
	36	0.000	0.255	0.529	0.852	1.052	1.306	1.688	2.028	2.434	2.719	3.333
	37	0.000	0.255	0.529	0.851	1.051	1.305	1.687	2.026	2.431	2.715	3.326
	38	0.000	0.255	0.529	0.851	1.051	1.304	1.686	2.024	2.429	2.712	3.319
	39	0.000	0.255	0.529	0.851	1.050	1.304	1.685	2.023	2.426	2.708	3.313
	40	0.000	0.255	0.529	0.851	1.050	1.303	1.684	2.021	2.423	2.704	3.307

t-Verteilung: Quantilsfunktion $Q_t(q;n)$ (Fortsetzung)

		Quantil q									
		0.500	0.600	0.700	0.800	0.850	0.900	0.950	0.975	0.990	0.995	0.999
Freiheitsgrade n	45	0.000	0.255	0.528	0.850	1.049	1.301	1.679	2.014	2.412	2.690	3.281
	50	0.000	0.255	0.528	0.849	1.047	1.299	1.676	2.009	2.403	2.678	3.261
	55	0.000	0.255	0.527	0.848	1.046	1.297	1.673	2.004	2.396	2.668	3.245
	60	0.000	0.254	0.527	0.848	1.045	1.296	1.671	2.000	2.390	2.660	3.232
	65	0.000	0.254	0.527	0.847	1.045	1.295	1.669	1.997	2.385	2.654	3.220
	70	0.000	0.254	0.527	0.847	1.044	1.294	1.667	1.994	2.381	2.648	3.211
	75	0.000	0.254	0.527	0.846	1.044	1.293	1.665	1.992	2.377	2.643	3.202
	80	0.000	0.254	0.526	0.846	1.043	1.292	1.664	1.990	2.374	2.639	3.195
	85	0.000	0.254	0.526	0.846	1.043	1.292	1.663	1.988	2.371	2.635	3.189
	90	0.000	0.254	0.526	0.846	1.042	1.291	1.662	1.987	2.368	2.632	3.183
	95	0.000	0.254	0.526	0.845	1.042	1.291	1.661	1.985	2.366	2.629	3.178
	100	0.000	0.254	0.526	0.845	1.042	1.290	1.660	1.984	2.364	2.626	3.174
	110	0.000	0.254	0.526	0.845	1.041	1.289	1.659	1.982	2.361	2.621	3.166
	120	0.000	0.254	0.526	0.845	1.041	1.289	1.658	1.980	2.358	2.617	3.160
	130	0.000	0.254	0.526	0.844	1.041	1.288	1.657	1.978	2.355	2.614	3.154
	140	0.000	0.254	0.526	0.844	1.040	1.288	1.656	1.977	2.353	2.611	3.149
	150	0.000	0.254	0.526	0.844	1.040	1.287	1.655	1.976	2.351	2.609	3.145
	160	0.000	0.254	0.525	0.844	1.040	1.287	1.654	1.975	2.350	2.607	3.142
	170	0.000	0.254	0.525	0.844	1.040	1.287	1.654	1.974	2.348	2.605	3.139
	180	0.000	0.254	0.525	0.844	1.039	1.286	1.653	1.973	2.347	2.603	3.136
	190	0.000	0.254	0.525	0.844	1.039	1.286	1.653	1.973	2.346	2.602	3.134
	200	0.000	0.254	0.525	0.843	1.039	1.286	1.653	1.972	2.345	2.601	3.131
	250	0.000	0.254	0.525	0.843	1.039	1.285	1.651	1.969	2.341	2.596	3.123
	300	0.000	0.254	0.525	0.843	1.038	1.284	1.650	1.968	2.339	2.592	3.118
	350	0.000	0.254	0.525	0.843	1.038	1.284	1.649	1.967	2.337	2.590	3.114
	400	0.000	0.254	0.525	0.843	1.038	1.284	1.649	1.966	2.336	2.588	3.111
	450	0.000	0.253	0.525	0.842	1.038	1.283	1.648	1.965	2.335	2.587	3.108
	500	0.000	0.253	0.525	0.842	1.038	1.283	1.648	1.965	2.334	2.586	3.107
	550	0.000	0.253	0.525	0.842	1.037	1.283	1.648	1.964	2.333	2.585	3.105
	600	0.000	0.253	0.525	0.842	1.037	1.283	1.647	1.964	2.333	2.584	3.104
	650	0.000	0.253	0.525	0.842	1.037	1.283	1.647	1.964	2.332	2.583	3.103
	700	0.000	0.253	0.525	0.842	1.037	1.283	1.647	1.963	2.332	2.583	3.102
	750	0.000	0.253	0.525	0.842	1.037	1.283	1.647	1.963	2.331	2.582	3.101
	800	0.000	0.253	0.525	0.842	1.037	1.283	1.647	1.963	2.331	2.582	3.100
	850	0.000	0.253	0.525	0.842	1.037	1.283	1.647	1.963	2.331	2.582	3.100
	900	0.000	0.253	0.525	0.842	1.037	1.282	1.647	1.963	2.330	2.581	3.099
	950	0.000	0.253	0.525	0.842	1.037	1.282	1.646	1.962	2.330	2.581	3.099
	1000	0.000	0.253	0.525	0.842	1.037	1.282	1.646	1.962	2.330	2.581	3.098
	2000	0.000	0.253	0.524	0.842	1.037	1.282	1.646	1.961	2.328	2.578	3.094
	5000	0.000	0.253	0.524	0.842	1.037	1.282	1.645	1.960	2.327	2.577	3.092
	∞	0.000	0.253	0.524	0.842	1.036	1.282	1.645	1.960	2.326	2.576	3.090

6 R Befehle

6.1 Grundlegende R Befehle

Grundlagen:
`setwd("Pfad")`	Arbeitsverzeichnis
`library(Paket)`	Aktiviere Paket
`ls()`	Liste der aktuellen Variablen (Objekte)
`rm(v)`	Lösche Variable v aus dem Speicher
`rm(list=ls())`	Lösche *alle* Variablen aus dem Speicher

Allgemeine mathematische Funktionen:
`abs(v)`	Absolutwert (Betrag) $\|v\|$
`choose(n,k)`	Binomialkoeffizient $\binom{n}{k}$
`exp(v)`	Exponentialfunktion e^v
`factorial(n)`	Fakultät $n!$
`log(v)`	Natürlicher Logarithmus $\ln(v)$
`round(v,s)`	Runde v auf s Stellen
`sqrt(v)`	Quadratwurzel von v

Vektoren:
`c(x1,x2,...)`	Erzeuge einen Vektor mit den Werten x1,x2,...
`sort(v)`	Sortierte Werte
`cbind(v1,v2,...)`	Ausgabe der Vektoren v1,v2,... als Spalten nebeneinander
`rbind(v1,v2,...)`	Ausgabe der Vektoren v1,v2,... als Zeilen untereinander
`length(v)`	Länge des Vektors v
`unique(v)`	Unterschiedliche Werte, Ausprägungsliste
`sum(v)`	Summe aller Elemente des Vektors v
`cumsum(v)`	Kumulative Summe aller Elemente des Vektors v
`prod(v)`	Produkt aller Elemente des Vektors v
`max(v), min(v)`	Größter / Kleinster Wert des Vektors v
`table(v)`	Absolute Häufigkeiten für Vektor v
`table(v1,v2)`	Gemeinsame absolute Häufigkeiten
`prop.table(tab)`	Relative aus absoluten Häufigkeiten
`prop.table(tab,i)`	Rel. Häufigkeiten bedingt auf Zeile (i=1) oder Spalte (i=2)

Datensätze und Dateien:
`data.frame(v1,v2,...)`	Ausgabe der Vektoren v1,v2,... als Datensatz
`load("Dateiname")`	Lade R-Datensatz (*.RData)
`save("Dateiname")`	Speichere R-Datensatz (*.RData)
`import("Dateiname")`	Importiere Datensatz (Paket `rio`)
`ncol(df), nrow(df)`	Zahl der Spalten / Zeilen
`names(df)`	Namen der Variablen (Spalten)
`head(df), tail(df)`	Erste / Letzte 6 Zeilen des Datensatzes/Objektes
`with(df, ausdruck)`	Berechne `ausdruck` für Spalten des Datensatzes `df`

Sonstige Funktionen:
`for (r in 1:R){...}`	Wiederholung für alle Werte r=1,...,R
`numeric(Zahl)`	Erzeuge einen numerischen Vektor der Länge `Zahl`
`factor(v)`	Erzeuge eine explizit diskrete Variable
`cut(x, breaks, ...)`	Ordne `x`-Werte den Klassen zu, die mit `breaks` definiert wurden

Statistische Funktionen:

`mean(v)`	Arithmetisches Mittel des Vektors v
`quantile(v,q,type=1)`	q-Quantil des Vektors v, z.B. x_{Med}= `quantile(x,0.5,type=1)`
`median(v)`	Alternative Definition x^*_{Med}, identisch zu `quantile(x,0.5,type=7)`
`var(v), sd(v)`	Korrigierte Varianz / Standardabweichung von v
`cor(v1,v2)`	Korrelationskoeffizient
`cov(v1,v2)`	Korrigierte Kovarianz
`Lc(v)`	Lorenzkurve (Paket `ineq`)
`Gini(v)`	Gini-Koeffizient (Paket `ineq`)
`sample(GG,n,...)`	Ziehe ohne oder mit (`replace=TRUE`) Zurücklegen
`set.seed(`*Zahl*`)`	Setze den Zufallsgenerator auf Startwert *Zahl*
`t.test(v,mu=`*Wert*`)`	t-Test der Nullhypothese $H_0 : \mu_v =$ *Wert* (bei Normalverteilung)
	Optionen: `alternative="greater"` oder `"less"`, `conf.level=`*Wert*
`shapiro.test(`*variable*`)`	Shapiro-Wilk Test der Normalverteilung von *variable*
`chisq.test(`*n,p*`)`	Anpassungstest für abs. Häufigkeiten *n* und hyp. W'keiten *p* (optional)
`chisq.test(`*Tabelle*`)`	Unabhängigkeitstest für Kontingenztabelle *Tabelle*
`erg<-lm(y~x)`	Durchführung der linearen Regression, Ergebnisse in `erg`
`coef(erg)`	Koeffizienten als Vektor
`residuals(erg)`	Residuen als Vektor
`summary(erg)`	Ausgabe der relevantesten Ergebnisse

6.2 Beispiel-Code für Monte-Carlo Simulation

```
set.seed(123456)
mw <- numeric(10000)
teststat <- numeric(10000)
for (r in 1:10000) {
  SP <- rnorm(100, 0.3, 1)
  mw[r]<- mean(SP)
  teststat[r] <- sqrt(100) * (mean(SP)-0.1) / sd(SP)
}
mean(mw)
sd(mw)
verwerfen <- (abs(teststat) > 2)
table(verwerfen)
```

Data Visualization with ggplot2 :: CHEAT SHEET

Basics

ggplot2 is based on the **grammar of graphics**, the idea that you can build every graph from the same components: a **data** set, a **coordinate system**, and **geoms**—visual marks that represent data points.

data + geom + coordinate system = plot

To display values, map variables in the data to visual properties of the geom (**aesthetics**) like **size**, **color**, and **x** and **y** locations.

data + geom (color=F, size=A, x=F, y=A) + coordinate system = plot

Complete the template below to build a graph.

```
ggplot (data = <DATA>) +                              [required]
   <GEOM_FUNCTION> (mapping = aes(<MAPPINGS>),
   stat = <STAT>, position = <POSITION>) +            Not
   <COORDINATE_FUNCTION> +                            required,
   <FACET_FUNCTION> +                                 sensible
   <SCALE_FUNCTION> +                                 defaults
   <THEME_FUNCTION>                                   supplied
```

aesthetic mappings   data   geom

ggplot(data = mpg, aes(x = cty, y = hwy)) Begins a plot that you finish by adding layers to. Add one geom function per layer.

qplot(x = cty, y = hwy, data = mpg, geom = "point") Creates a complete plot with given data, geom, and mappings. Supplies many useful defaults.

last_plot() Returns the last plot

ggsave("plot.png", width = 5, height = 5) Saves last plot as 5' x 5' file named "plot.png" in working directory. Matches file type to file extension.

Geoms
Use a geom function to represent data points, use the geom's aesthetic properties to represent variables. Each function returns a layer.

GRAPHICAL PRIMITIVES

```
a <- ggplot(economics, aes(date, unemploy))
b <- ggplot(seals, aes(x = long, y = lat))
```

a + geom_blank()
(Useful for expanding limits)

b + geom_curve(aes(yend = lat + 1, xend=long+1,curvature=z)) - x, xend, y, yend, alpha, angle, color, curvature, linetype, size

a + geom_path(lineend="butt", linejoin="round", linemitre=1)
x, y, alpha, color, group, linetype, size

a + geom_polygon(aes(group = group))
x, y, alpha, color, fill, group, linetype, size

b + geom_rect(aes(xmin = long, ymin=lat, xmax= long + 1, ymax = lat +1)) - xmax, xmin, ymax, ymin, alpha, color, fill, linetype, size

a + geom_ribbon(aes(ymin=unemploy - 900, ymax=unemploy + 900)) - x, ymax, ymin, alpha, color, fill, group, linetype, size

LINE SEGMENTS
common aesthetics: x, y, alpha, color, linetype, size

b + geom_abline(aes(intercept=0, slope=1))
b + geom_hline(aes(yintercept = lat))
b + geom_vline(aes(xintercept = long))
b + geom_segment(aes(yend=lat+1, xend=long+1))
b + geom_spoke(aes(angle = 1:1155, radius = 1))

ONE VARIABLE   continuous
c <- ggplot(mpg, aes(hwy)); c2 <- ggplot(mpg)

c + geom_area(stat = "bin")
x, y, alpha, color, fill, linetype, size

c + geom_density(kernel = "gaussian")
x, y, alpha, color, fill, group, linetype, size, weight

c + geom_dotplot()
x, y, alpha, color, fill

c + geom_freqpoly() x, y, alpha, color, group, linetype, size

c + geom_histogram(binwidth = 5) x, y, alpha, color, fill, linetype, size, weight

c2 + geom_qq(aes(sample = hwy)) x, y, alpha, color, fill, linetype, size, weight

discrete

d <- ggplot(mpg, aes(fl))

d + geom_bar()
x, alpha, color, fill, linetype, size, weight

TWO VARIABLES

continuous x , continuous y
e <- ggplot(mpg, aes(cty, hwy))

e + geom_label(aes(label = cty), nudge_x = 1, nudge_y = 1, check_overlap = TRUE) x, y, label, alpha, angle, color, family, fontface, hjust, lineheight, size, vjust

e + geom_jitter(height = 2, width = 2)
x, y, alpha, color, fill, shape, size

e + geom_point(), x, y, alpha, color, fill, shape, size, stroke

e + geom_quantile(), x, y, alpha, color, group, linetype, size, weight

e + geom_rug(sides = "bl"), x, y, alpha, color, linetype, size

e + geom_smooth(method = lm), x, y, alpha, color, fill, group, linetype, size, weight

e + geom_text(aes(label = cty), nudge_x = 1, nudge_y = 1, check_overlap = TRUE) x, y, label, alpha, angle, color, family, fontface, hjust, lineheight, size, vjust

discrete x , continuous y
f <- ggplot(mpg, aes(class, hwy))

f + geom_col(), x, y, alpha, color, fill, group, linetype, size

f + geom_boxplot(), x, y, alpha, color, fill, group, linetype, shape, size, weight

f + geom_dotplot(binaxis = "y", stackdir = "center"), x, y, alpha, color, fill, group

f + geom_violin(scale = "area"), x, y, alpha, color, fill, group, linetype, size, weight

discrete x , discrete y
g <- ggplot(diamonds, aes(cut, color))

g + geom_count(), x, y, alpha, color, fill, shape, size, stroke

THREE VARIABLES

seals$z <- with(seals, sqrt(delta_long^2 + delta_lat^2))l <- ggplot(seals, aes(long, lat))

l + geom_contour(aes(z = z))
x, y, z, alpha, colour, group, linetype, size, weight

continuous bivariate distribution
h <- ggplot(diamonds, aes(carat, price))

h + geom_bin2d(binwidth = c(0.25, 500))
x, y, alpha, color, fill, linetype, size, weight

h + geom_density2d()
x, y, alpha, colour, group, linetype, size

h + geom_hex()
x, y, alpha, colour, fill, size

continuous function
i <- ggplot(economics, aes(date, unemploy))

i + geom_area()
x, y, alpha, color, fill, linetype, size

i + geom_line()
x, y, alpha, color, group, linetype, size

i + geom_step(direction = "hv")
x, y, alpha, color, group, linetype, size

visualizing error
df <- data.frame(grp = c("A", "B"), fit = 4:5, se = 1:2)
j <- ggplot(df, aes(grp, fit, ymin = fit-se, ymax = fit+se))

j + geom_crossbar(fatten = 2)
x, y, ymax, ymin, alpha, color, fill, group, linetype, size

j + geom_errorbar(), x, ymax, ymin, alpha, color, group, linetype, size, width (also geom_errorbarh())

j + geom_linerange()
x, ymin, ymax, alpha, color, group, linetype, size

j + geom_pointrange()
x, y, ymin, ymax, alpha, color, fill, group, linetype, shape, size

maps
data <- data.frame(murder = USArrests$Murder, state = tolower(rownames(USArrests)))
map <- map_data("state")
k <- ggplot(data, aes(fill = murder))

k + geom_map(aes(map_id = state), map = map) + **expand_limits**(x = map$long, y = map$lat), map_id, alpha, color, fill, linetype, size

l + geom_raster(aes(fill = z), hjust=0.5, vjust=0.5, interpolate=FALSE), x, y, alpha, color, fill

l + geom_tile(aes(fill = z)), x, y, alpha, color, fill, linetype, size, width

RStudio® is a trademark of RStudio, Inc. • CC BY SA RStudio • info@rstudio.com • 844-448-1212 • rstudio.com • Learn more at **http://ggplot2.tidyverse.org** • ggplot2 2.1.0 • Updated: 2016-11

ggplot2

Stats — An alternative way to build a layer

A stat builds new variables to plot (e.g., count, prop).

Visualize a stat by changing the default stat of a geom function, **geom_bar(stat="count")** or by using a stat function, **stat_count(geom="bar")**, which calls a default geom to make a layer (equivalent to a geom function). Use **..name..** syntax to map stat variables to aesthetics.

```
i + stat_density2d(aes(fill = ..level..),
                   geom = "polygon")
```

c + **stat_bin**(binwidth = 1, origin = 10)
x, y | ..count.., ..ncount.., ..density.., ..ndensity..

c + **stat_count**(width = 1) x, y | ..count.., ..prop..

c + **stat_density**(adjust = 1, kernel = "gaussian")
x, y | ..count.., ..density.., ..scaled..

e + **stat_bin_2d**(bins = 30, drop = T)
x, y, fill | ..count.., ..density..

e + **stat_bin_hex**(bins=30) x, y, fill | ..count.., ..density..

e + **stat_density_2d**(contour = TRUE, n = 100)
x, y, color, size | ..level..

e + **stat_ellipse**(level = 0.95, segments = 51, type = "t")

l + **stat_contour**(aes(z = z)) x, y, z, order | ..level..

l + **stat_summary_hex**(aes(z = z), bins = 30, fun = max)
x, y, z, fill | ..value..

l + **stat_summary_2d**(aes(z = z), bins = 30, fun = mean)
x, y, z, fill | ..value..

f + **stat_boxplot**(coef = 1.5) x, y | ..lower.., ..middle.., ..upper.., ..width.., ..ymin.., ..ymax..

f + **stat_ydensity**(kernel = "gaussian", scale = "area") x, y | ..density.., ..scaled.., ..count.., ..n.., ..violinwidth.., ..width..

e + **stat_ecdf**(n = 40) x, y | ..x.., ..y..

e + **stat_quantile**(quantiles = c(0.1, 0.9), formula = y ~ log(x), method = "rq") x, y | ..quantile..

e + **stat_smooth**(method = "lm", formula = y ~ x, se=T, level=0.95) x, y | ..se.., ..x.., ..y.., ..ymin.., ..ymax..

ggplot() + **stat_function**(aes(x = -3:3), n = 99, fun = dnorm, args = list(sd=0.5)) x | ..x.., ..y..

e + **stat_identity**(na.rm = TRUE)

ggplot() + **stat_qq**(aes(sample=1:100), dist = qt, dparam=list(df=5)) sample, x, y | ..sample.., ..theoretical..

e + **stat_sum**() x, y, size | ..n.., ..prop..

e + **stat_summary**(fun.data = "mean_cl_boot")

h + **stat_summary_bin**(fun.y = "mean", geom = "bar")

e + **stat_unique**()

Scales

Scales map data values to the visual values of an aesthetic. To change a mapping, add a new scale.

(n <- d + geom_bar(aes(fill = fl))

n + **scale_fill_manual**(
  values = c("skyblue", "royalblue", "blue", "navy"),
  limits = c("d", "e", "p", "r"), breaks =c("d", "e", "p", "r"),
  name = "fuel", labels = c("D", "E", "P", "R"))

GENERAL PURPOSE SCALES
Use with most aesthetics

scale_*_continuous() - map cont' values to visual ones
scale_*_discrete() - map discrete values to visual ones
scale_*_identity() - use data values as visual ones
scale_*_manual(values = c()) - map discrete values to manually chosen visual ones
scale_*_date(date_labels = "%m/%d"), date_breaks = "2 weeks") - treat data values as dates.
scale_*_datetime() - treat data x values as date times.
Use same arguments as scale_x_date(). See ?strptime for label formats.

X & Y LOCATION SCALES
Use with x or y aesthetics (x shown here)

scale_x_log10() - Plot x on log10 scale
scale_x_reverse() - Reverse direction of x axis
scale_x_sqrt() - Plot x on square root scale

COLOR AND FILL SCALES (DISCRETE)

n <- d + geom_bar(aes(fill = fl))

n + **scale_fill_brewer**(palette = "Blues")
For palette choices:
RColorBrewer::display.brewer.all()

n + **scale_fill_grey**(start = 0.2, end = 0.8, na.value = "red")

COLOR AND FILL SCALES (CONTINUOUS)

o <- c + geom_dotplot(aes(fill = ..x..))

o + **scale_fill_distiller**(palette = "Blues")

o + **scale_fill_gradient**(low="red", high="yellow")

o + **scale_fill_gradient2**(low="red", high="blue", mid = "white", midpoint = 25)

o + **scale_fill_gradientn**(colours=topo.colors(6))
Also: rainbow(), heat.colors(), terrain.colors(), cm.colors(), RColorBrewer::brewer.pal()

SHAPE AND SIZE SCALES

p <- e + geom_point(aes(shape = fl, size = cyl))
p + **scale_shape**() + **scale_size**()
p + **scale_shape_manual**(values = c(3:7))
p + **scale_radius**(range = c(1,6))
p + **scale_size_area**(max_size = 6)

Coordinate Systems

r <- d + geom_bar()

r + **coord_cartesian**(xlim = c(0, 5))
The default cartesian coordinate system

r + **coord_fixed**(ratio = 1/2)
Cartesian coordinates with fixed aspect ratio between x and y units

r + **coord_flip**()
xlim, ylim
Flipped Cartesian coordinates

r + **coord_polar**(theta = "x", direction=1)
theta, start, direction
Polar coordinates

r + **coord_trans**(ytrans = "sqrt")
xtrans, ytrans, limx, limy
Transformed cartesian Coordinates. Set xtrans and ytrans to the name of a window function.

π + **coord_quickmap**()
π + **coord_map**(projection = "ortho", orientation=c(41, -74, 0))projection, orientation, xlim, ylim
Map projections from the mapproj package (mercator (default), azequalarea, lagrange, etc.)

Position Adjustments

Position adjustments determine how to arrange geoms that would otherwise occupy the same space.

s <- ggplot(mpg, aes(fl, fill = drv))

s + **geom_bar**(position = "dodge")
Arrange elements side by side

s + **geom_bar**(position = "fill")
Stack elements on top of one another, normalize height

e + **geom_point**(position = "jitter")
Add random noise to X and Y position of each element to avoid overplotting

e + **geom_label**(position = "nudge")
Nudge labels away from points

s + **geom_bar**(position = "stack")
Stack elements on top of one another

Each position adjustment can be recast as a function with manual **width** and **height** arguments
s + geom_bar(position = position_dodge(width = 1))

Faceting

Facets divide a plot into subplots based on the values of one or more discrete variables.

t <- ggplot(mpg, aes(cty, hwy)) + geom_point()

t + **facet_grid**(. ~ fl)
facet into columns based on fl

t + **facet_grid**(year ~ .)
facet into rows based on year

t + **facet_grid**(year ~ fl)
facet into both rows and columns

t + **facet_wrap**(~ fl)
wrap facets into a rectangular layout

Set scales to let axis limits vary across facets

t + **facet_grid**(drv ~ fl, scales = "free")
x and y axis limits adjust to individual facets
"free_x" - x axis limits adjust
"free_y" - y axis limits adjust

Set **labeller** to adjust facet labels

t + **facet_grid**(. ~ fl, labeller = label_both)
fl: c   fl: d   fl: e   fl: p   fl: r

t + **facet_grid**(. ~ fl, labeller = label_bquote(alpha ^ .(fl)))
α^c α^d α^e α^p α^r

t + **facet_grid**(. ~ fl, labeller = label_parsed)

Labels

t + **labs**(x = "New x axis label", y = "New y axis label",
  title = "Add a title above the plot",
  subtitle = "Add a subtitle below title",
  caption = "Add a caption below plot")

n + **guides**(fill = "none")
Set legend type for each aesthetic: colorbar, legend, or none (no legend)

n + **scale_fill_discrete**(name = "Title",
  labels = c("A", "B", "C", "D", "E"))
Set legend title and labels with a scale function.

t + **annotate**(geom = "text", x = 8, y = 9, label = "A")

Legends

n + **theme**(legend.position = "bottom")
Place legend at "bottom", "top", "left", or "right"

Zooming

Without clipping (preferred)

t + **coord_cartesian**(
  xlim = c(0, 100), ylim = c(10, 20))

With clipping (removes unseen data points)

t + **xlim**(0, 100) + **ylim**(10, 20)

t + **scale_x_continuous**(limits = c(0, 100)) +
scale_y_continuous(limits = c(0, 100))

Themes

r + **theme_bw**()
White background with grid lines

r + **theme_gray**()
Grey background (default theme)

r + **theme_dark**()
dark for contrast

r + **theme_classic**()

r + **theme_light**()

r + **theme_linedraw**()

r + **theme_minimal**()
Minimal themes

r + **theme_void**()
Empty theme

Data Transformation with dplyr :: CHEAT SHEET

dplyr functions work with pipes and expect **tidy data**. In tidy data:

- Each **variable** is in its own **column**
- Each **observation**, or **case**, is in its own **row**

pipes
x %>% f(y) becomes f(x, y)

Manipulate Variables

EXTRACT VARIABLES

Column functions return a set of columns as a new table. Use a variant that ends in _ for non-standard evaluation friendly code.

select(.data, ...) Extract columns by name. Also **select_if()**
select(iris, Sepal.Length, Species)

Use these helpers with select (),
e.g. select(iris, starts_with("Sepal"))

- **contains**(match)
- **ends_with**(match)
- **matches**(match)
- **num_range**(prefix, range)
- **one_of**(...)
- **starts_with**(match)

:, e.g. mpg:cyl
-, e.g. -Species

MAKE NEW VARIABLES

These apply **vectorized functions** to columns. Vectorized funs take vectors as input and return vectors of the same length as output (see back).

vectorized function

mutate(.data, ...)
Compute new column(s).
mutate(mtcars, gpm = 1/mpg)

transmute(.data, ...)
Compute new column(s), drop others.
transmute(mtcars, gpm = 1/mpg)

mutate_all(.tbl, .funs, ...) Apply funs to every column. Use with **funs()**.
mutate_all(faithful, funs(log(.), log2(.)))

mutate_at(.tbl, .cols, .funs, ...) Apply funs to specific columns. Use with **funs()**, **vars()** and the helper functions for select().
mutate_at(iris, vars(-Species), funs(log(.)))

mutate_if(.tbl, .predicate, .funs, ...)
Apply funs to all columns of one type.
Use with **funs()**.
mutate_if(iris, is.numeric, funs(log(.)))

add_column(.data, ..., .before = NULL, .after = NULL) Add new column(s).
add_column(mtcars, new = 1:32)

rename(.data, ...) Rename columns.
rename(iris, Length = Sepal.Length)

Manipulate Cases

EXTRACT CASES

Row functions return a subset of rows as a new table. Use a variant that ends in _ for non-standard evaluation friendly code.

filter(.data, ...) Extract rows that meet logical criteria. Also **filter_()**. *filter(iris, Sepal.Length > 7)*

distinct(.data, ..., .keep_all = FALSE) Remove rows with duplicate values. Also **distinct_()**.
distinct(iris, Species)

sample_frac(tbl, size = 1, replace = FALSE, weight = NULL, .env = parent.frame()) Randomly select fraction of rows.
sample_frac(iris, 0.5, replace = TRUE)

sample_n(tbl, size, replace = FALSE, weight = NULL, .env = parent.frame()) Randomly select size rows. *sample_n(iris, 10, replace = TRUE)*

slice(.data, ...) Select rows by position. Also **slice_()**. *slice(iris, 10:15)*

top_n(x, n, wt) Select and order top n entries (by group if grouped data). *top_n(iris, 5, Sepal.Width)*

Logical and boolean operators to use with filter()

| < | <= | is.na() | %in% | | | xor() |
| > | >= | !is.na() | ! | & | \| | |

See **?base::logic** and **?Comparison** for help.

ARRANGE CASES

arrange(.data, ...) Order rows by values of a column or columns (low to high), use with **desc()** to order from high to low.
arrange(mtcars, mpg)
arrange(mtcars, desc(mpg))

ADD CASES

add_row(.data,..., .before = NULL, .after = NULL) Add one or more rows to a table.
add_row(faithful, eruptions = 1, waiting = 1)

Summarise Cases

These apply **summary functions** to columns to create a new table. Summary functions take vectors as input and return one value (see back).

summary function

summarise(.data, ...)
Compute table of summaries. Also **summarise_()**.
summarise(mtcars, avg = mean(mpg))

count(x, ..., wt = NULL, sort = FALSE)
Count number of rows in each group defined by the variables in ... Also **tally()**.
count(iris, Species)

VARIATIONS

summarise_all() - Apply funs to every column.
summarise_at() - Apply funs to specific columns.
summarise_if() - Apply funs to all cols of one type.

Group Cases

Use **group_by()** to create a "grouped" copy of a table. dplyr functions will manipulate each "group" separately and then combine the results.

mtcars %>%
group_by(cyl) %>%
summarise(avg = mean(mpg))

group_by(.data, ..., add = FALSE)
Returns copy of table grouped by ...
g_iris <- group_by(iris, Species)

ungroup(x, ...)
Returns ungrouped copy of table.
ungroup(g_iris)

RStudio® is a trademark of RStudio, Inc. • CC BY SA RStudio • info@rstudio.com • 844-448-1212 • rstudio.com • Learn more with browseVignettes(package = c("dplyr", "tibble")) • dplyr 0.5.0 • tibble 1.2.0 • Updated: 2017-01

Vector Functions

TO USE WITH MUTATE ()

mutate() and **transmute()** apply vectorized functions to columns to create new columns. Vectorized functions take vectors as input and return vectors of the same length as output.

vectorized function

OFFSETS
dplyr::**lag()** - Offset elements by 1
dplyr::**lead()** - Offset elements by -1

CUMULATIVE AGGREGATES
dplyr::**cumall()** - Cumulative all()
dplyr::**cumany()** - Cumulative any()
dplyr::**cummax()** - Cumulative max()
dplyr::**cummean()** - Cumulative mean()
cummin() - Cumulative min()
cumprod() - Cumulative prod()
cumsum() - Cumulative sum()

RANKINGS
dplyr::**cume_dist()** - Proportion of all values <=
dplyr::**dense_rank()** - rank with ties = min, no gaps
dplyr::**min_rank()** - rank with ties = min
dplyr::**ntile()** - bins into n bins
dplyr::**percent_rank()** - min_rank scaled to [0,1]
dplyr::**row_number()** - rank with ties = "first"

MATH
+, -, *, /, ^, %/%, %% - arithmetic ops
log(), log2(), log10() - logs
<, <=, >, >=, !=, == - logical comparisons

MISC
dplyr::**between()** - x >= left & x <= right
dplyr::**case_when()** - multi-case if_else()
dplyr::**coalesce()** - first non-NA values by element across a set of vectors
dplyr::**if_else()** - element-wise if() + else()
dplyr::**na_if()** - replace specific values with NA
pmax() - element-wise max()
pmin() - element-wise min()
dplyr::**recode()** - Vectorized switch()
dplyr::**recode_factor()** - Vectorized switch() for factors

Summary Functions

TO USE WITH SUMMARISE ()

summarise() applies summary functions to columns to create a new table. Summary functions take vectors as input and return single values as output.

summary function

COUNTS
dplyr::**n()** - number of values/rows
dplyr::**n_distinct()** - # of uniques
sum(!is.na()) - # of non-NA's

LOCATION
mean() - mean, also **mean(!is.na())**
median() - median

LOGICALS
mean() - Proportion of TRUE's
sum() - # of TRUE's

POSITION/ORDER
dplyr::**first()** - first value
dplyr::**last()** - last value
dplyr::**nth()** - value in nth location of vector

RANK
quantile() - nth quantile
min() - minimum value
max() - maximum value

SPREAD
IQR() - Inter-Quartile Range
mad() - median absolute deviation
sd() - standard deviation
var() - variance

Combine Tables

COMBINE VARIABLES

Use **bind_cols()** to paste tables beside each other as they are.

bind_cols(...) Returns tables placed side by side as a single table.
BE SURE THAT ROWS ALIGN.

Use a "**Mutating Join**" to join one table to columns from another, matching values with the rows that they correspond to. Each join retains a different combination of values from the tables.

left_join(x, y, by = NULL, copy=FALSE, suffix=c(".x",".y"),...)
Join matching values from y to x.

right_join(x, y, by = NULL, copy = FALSE, suffix=c(".x",".y"),...)
Join matching values from x to y.

inner_join(x, y, by = NULL, copy = FALSE, suffix=c(".x",".y"),...)
Join data. Retain only rows with matches.

full_join(x, y, by = NULL, copy=FALSE, suffix=c(".x",".y"),...)
Join data. Retain all values, all rows.

Use **by = c("col1", "col2")** to specify the column(s) to match on. *left_join(x, y, by = "A")*

Use a named vector, **by = c("col1" = "col2")**, to match on columns with different names in each data set. *left_join(x, y, by = c("C" = "D"))*

Use **suffix** to specify suffix to give to duplicate column names. *left_join(x, y, by = c("C" = "D"), suffix = c(".1", ".2"))*

Row Names

Tidy data does not use rownames, which store a variable outside of the columns. To work with the rownames, first move them into a column.

rownames_to_column()
Move row names into col.
a <- rownames_to_column(iris, var = "C")

column_to_rownames()
Move col in row names.
column_to_rownames(a, var = "C")

Also **has_rownames()**, **remove_rownames()**

COMBINE CASES

Use **bind_rows()** to paste tables below each other as they are.

bind_rows(..., .id = NULL)
Returns tables one on top of the other as a single table. Set .id to a column name to add a column of the original table names (as pictured)

intersect(x, y, ...)
Rows that appear in both x and y.

setdiff(x, y, ...)
Rows that appear in x but not y.

union(x, y, ...)
Rows that appear in x or y. (Duplicates removed). union_all() retains duplicates.

Use **setequal()** to test whether two data sets contain the exact same rows (in any order).

EXTRACT ROWS

Use a "**Filtering Join**" to filter one table against the rows of another.

semi_join(x, y, by = NULL, ...)
Return rows of x that have a match in y.
USEFUL TO SEE WHAT WILL BE JOINED.

anti_join(x, y, by = NULL, ...)
Return rows of x that do not have a match in y. USEFUL TO SEE WHAT WILL NOT BE JOINED.

R Markdown :: CHEAT SHEET

What is R Markdown?

.Rmd files · An R Markdown (.Rmd) file is a record of your research. It contains the code that a scientist needs to reproduce your work along with the narration that a reader needs to understand your work.

Reproducible Research · At the click of a button, or the type of a command, you can rerun the code in an R Markdown file to reproduce your work and export the results as a finished report.

Dynamic Documents · You can choose to export the finished report in a variety of formats, including html, pdf, MS Word, or RTF documents; html or pdf based slides, Notebooks, and more.

Workflow

1. **Open a new .Rmd file** at File ▶ New File ▶ R Markdown. Use the wizard that opens to pre-populate the file with a template
2. **Write document** by editing template
3. **Knit document to create report**; use knit button or render() to knit
4. **Preview Output** in IDE window
5. **Publish** (optional) to web server
6. **Examine build log** in R Markdown console
7. **Use output file** that is saved along side .Rmd

Embed code with knitr syntax

INLINE CODE
Insert with `` `r <code>` ``. Results appear as text without code.
Built with `r getRversion()`   Built with 3.2.3

CODE CHUNKS
One or more lines surrounded with ```` ``` ```` ``` {r} ``` and ```` ``` ````. Place chunk options within curly braces, after r. Insert with

```
{r include=FALSE}
getRversion()
```
[1] '3.2.3'

IMPORTANT CHUNK OPTIONS

cache - cache results for future knits (default = FALSE)

cache.path - directory to save cached results in (default = "cache/")

child - file(s) to knit and then include (default = NULL)

collapse - collapse all output into single block (default = FALSE)

comment - prefix for each line of results (default = '##')

dependson - chunk dependencies for caching (default = NULL)

echo - Display code in output document (default = TRUE)

engine - code language used in chunk (default = 'R')

error - Display error messages in doc (TRUE) or stop render when errors occur (FALSE) (default = FALSE)

eval - Run code in chunk (default = TRUE)

fig.align - 'left', 'right', or 'center' (default = 'default')

fig.cap - figure caption as character string (default = NULL)

fig.height, fig.width - Dimensions of plots in inches

highlight - highlight source code (default = TRUE)

include - Include chunk in doc after running (default = TRUE)

message - display code messages in document (default = TRUE)

results (default = 'markup')
'asis' - passthrough results
'hide' - do not display results
'hold' - put all results below all code

tidy - tidy code for display (default = FALSE)

warning - display code warnings in document (default = TRUE)

Options not listed above: R.options, aniopts, autodep, background, cache.comments, cache.lazy, cache.rebuild, cache.vars, dev, dev.args, dpi, engine.opts, engine.path, fig.asp, fig.env, fig.ext, fig.keep, fig.lp, fig.path, fig.pos, fig.process, fig.retina, fig.scap, fig.show, fig.showtext, fig.subcap, interval, out.extra, out.height, out.width, prompt, purl, ref.label, render, size, split, tidy.opts

render

Use markdown::**render()** to render/knit at cmd line. Important args:

input - file to render
output_format
output_options - List of render options (as in YAML)
output_file
output_dir
params - list of params to use
envir - environment to evaluate code chunks in
encoding - of input file

GLOBAL OPTIONS
Set with knitr::**opts_chunk$set()**, e.g.
knitr::opts_chunk$set(echo = TRUE)

.rmd Structure

YAML Header
Optional section of render (e.g. pandoc) options written as key-value pairs (YAML).
At start of file
Between lines of - - -

Text
Narration formatted with markdown, mixed with:

Code Chunks
Chunks of embedded code. Each chunk:
Begins with ``` ```{r} ```
ends with ``` ``` ```

R Markdown will run the code and append the results to the doc. It will use the location of the .Rmd file as the **working directory**

Parameters

Parameterize your documents to reuse with different inputs (e.g., data, values, etc.)

1. **Add parameters** - Create and set parameters in the header as sub-values of params
2. **Call parameters** - Call parameter values in code as params$<name>
3. **Set parameters** - Set values with Knit with parameters or the params argument of render():
render("doc.Rmd", params = list(n = 1, d = as.Date("2015-01-01")))

params:
n: 100
d: !r Sys.Date()

Today's date is `r params$d`

Knit HTML
Knit to HTML
Knit to PDF
Knit to Word
Knit with Parameters...

Interactive Documents

Turn your report into an interactive Shiny document in 4 steps

1. Add runtime: shiny to the YAML header.
2. Call Shiny input functions to embed input objects.
3. Call Shiny render functions to embed reactive output.
4. Render with rmarkdown::run or click Run Document in RStudio IDE

```
---
output: html_document
runtime: shiny
---

`` `{r, echo = FALSE}
numericInput("n",
  "How many cars?", 5)

renderTable({
  head(cars, input$n)
})
`` `
```

How many cars? 5

	speed	dist
1	4.00	2.00
2	4.00	10.00
3	7.00	4.00
4	7.00	22.00
5	8.00	16.00

Embed a complete app into your document with shiny::**shinyAppDir()**

NOTE: *Your report will rendered as a Shiny app, which means you must choose an html output format, like* **html_document**, *and serve it with an active R Session.*

RStudio® is a trademark of RStudio, Inc. • CC BY SA RStudio • info@rstudio.com • 844-448-1212 • rstudio.com • Learn more at rmarkdown.rstudio.com • rmarkdown 1.6 • Updated: 2016-02

rmarkdown

Pandoc's Markdown
Write with syntax on the left to create effect on right (after render)

Plain text
End a line with two spaces to start a new paragraph.
italics and **bold**
`verbatim code`
sub/superscript^2^~2~
~~strikethrough~~
escaped: *_\\
endash: --, emdash: ---
equation: $A = \pi*r^{2}$
equation block:

$$E = mc^2$$

> block quote

Header 1 {#anchor}
Header 2 {#css_id}
Header 3 {.css_class}
Header 4
Header 5
Header 6

<!--Text comment-->

\textbf[Tex ignored in HTML]
HTML ignored in pdfs

<http://www.rstudio.com>
[link](http://www.rstudio.com)
Jump to [Header 1](#anchor)

image:
![Caption](smallorb.png)

* unordered list
    + sub-item 1
    + sub-item 2
        - sub-sub-item 1

* item 2

    Continued (indent 4 spaces)

1. ordered list
2. item 2
    i) sub-item 1
        A. sub-sub-item 1

(@) A list whose numbering

continues after

(@) an interruption

Term 1
: Definition 1

Right	Left	Default	Center
12	12	12	12
123	123	123	123
1	1	1	1

- slide bullet 1
- slide bullet 2

(>- to have bullets appear on click)

horizontal rule/slide break:
***

A footnote [^1]

[^1]: Here is the footnote.

Set render options with YAML

When you render, R Markdown
1. runs the R code, embeds results and text into .md file with knitr
2. then converts the .md file into the finished format with pandoc

.Rmd → knitr → .md → pandoc → output

Set a document's default output format in the YAML header:

```
---
output: html_document
---
# Body
```

output value / creates

output value	creates
html_document	html
pdf_document	pdf (requires Tex)
word_document	Microsoft Word (.docx)
odt_document	OpenDocument Text
rtf_document	Rich Text Format
md_document	Markdown
github_document	Github compatible markdown
ioslides_presentation	ioslides HTML slides
slidy_presentation	slidy HTML slides
beamer_presentation	Beamer pdf slides (requires Tex)

Customize output with sub-options (listed to the right):

```
---
output: html_document:
    code_folding: hide
    toc_float: TRUE
---
# Body
```

html tabsets
Use tablet css class to place sub-headers into tabs

```
# Tabset {.tabset .tabset-fade .tabset-pills}
## Tab 1
text 1
## Tab 2
text 2
### End tabset
```

Tabset
| text 1 | End tabset |

sub-option — description

sub-option	description
citation_package	The LaTeX package to process citations, natbib, biblatex or none
code_folding	Let readers to toggle the display of R code, "none" "hide", or "show"
colortheme	Beamer color theme to use
css	CSS file to use to style document
dev	Graphics device to use for figure output (e.g. "png")
duration	Add a countdown timer (in minutes) to footer of slides
fig_caption	Should figures be rendered with captions?
fig_height, fig_width	Default figure height and width (in inches) for document
highlight	Syntax highlighting: "tango", "pygments", "kate", "zenburn", "textmate"
includes	File of content to place in document (in_header, before_body, after_body)
incremental	Should bullets appear one at a time (on presenter mouse clicks)?
keep_md	Save a copy of .md file that contains knitr output
keep_tex	Save a copy of .tex file that contains knitr output
latex_engine	Engine to render latex, "pdflatex", "xelatex", or "lualatex"
lib_dir	Directory of dependency files to use (Bootstrap, MathJax, etc.)
mathjax	Set to local or a URL to use a local/URL version of MathJax to render equations
md_extensions	Markdown extensions to add to default definition or R Markdown
number_sections	Add section numbering to headers
pandoc_args	Additional arguments to pass to Pandoc
preserve_yaml	Preserve YAML front matter in final document?
reference_docx	docx file whose styles should be copied when producing docx output
self_contained	Embed dependencies into the doc
slide_level	The lowest heading level that defines individual slides
smaller	Use the smaller font size in the presentation?
smart	Convert straight quotes to curly, dashes to em-dashes, ... to ellipses, etc.
template	Pandoc template to use when rendering file (quarterly_report.html).
theme	Bootswatch or Beamer theme to use for page
toc	Add a table of contents at start of document
toc_depth	The lowest level of headings to add to table of contents
toc_float	Float the table of contents to the left of the main content

Create a Reusable Template

1. **Create a new package**. Place a folder with a inst/rmarkdown/templates directory
2. In the directory, **Place a folder** that contains:
   template.yaml (see below)
   skeleton.Rmd (contents of the template)
   any supporting files
3. **Install the package**
4. **Access template** in wizard at File ▶ New File ▶ R Markdown

```
---
template.yaml
name: My Template
---
```

Table Suggestions

Several functions format R data into tables

	eruptions	waiting
1	3.600	79.00
2	1.800	54.00
3	3.333	74.00
4	2.283	62.00

```
data <- faithful[1:4,]
```

`knitr::kable(data, caption = "Table with kable")`
{r results = 'asis'}

`print(xtable::xtable(data, caption = "Table with xtable", type = "html", html.table.attributes = "border=0"))`
{r results = 'asis'}

`stargazer::stargazer(data, type = "html", title = "Table with stargazer")`
{r results = 'asis'}

Citations and Bibliographies

Create citations with .bib, .bibtex, .copac, .enl, .json, .medline, .mods, .ris, .wos, and .xml files

1. **Set bibliography file** and CSL 1.0
   Style file (optional) in the YAML header
   ```
   bibliography: refs.bib
   csl: style.csl
   ```
2. **Use citation keys in text**

   Smith cited [@smith04].
   Smith cited without author [-@smith04].
   @smith04 cited in line.

3. **Render.** Bibliography will be added to end of document

   Smith cited (Joe Smith 2004).
   Smith cited without author (2004).
   Joe Smith (2004) cited in line.

www.ingramcontent.com/pod-product-compliance
Lightning Source LLC
Chambersburg PA
CBHW062345220526
45469CB00008B/2845